CHINA BASICS SERIES

ETHNIC GROUPS IN CHINA

Author: Wang Can

Translator: Wang Pingxing

CHINA INTERCONTINENTAL PRESS

中国基本情况丛书

顾　　问　李　冰
主　　编　郭长建
副 主 编　宋坚之（执行）　吴　伟

责任编辑　冯凌宇　徐蔚然
装帧设计　方　红

图书在版编目(CIP)数据

中国民族／王灿著；王平兴译．－北京：
五洲传播出版社，2004.5
ISBN 7-5085-0490-9
I．中...
II．①王...②王...
III．中华民族—概况—英文
IV．K28

出版发行　五洲传播出版社（北京海淀区莲花池东路北小马厂6号　邮编：100038）
电　　话　8610-58891281（发行部）
网　　址　http://www.cicc.org.cn
设计制作　北京天人鉴设计制作有限公司
印　　刷　北京利丰雅高长城印刷有限公司
开　　本　889 × 1194毫米　1/32
字　　数　62千字
印　　张　5.375
版　　次　2004年5月第1版
印　　次　2006年10月第2次印刷
印　　数　7001-10000册
书　　号　ISBN 7-5085-0490-9/K·526
定　　价　54.00元

CONTENTS

PREFACE

Some people have asked me, "There are so many ethnic minorities in China. Could you give us a brief account of them?" This would be really a challenging task. To get to know China's ethnic minorities, usually one has to know some basic data: for instance, there are 55 minority ethnic groups in China, and the largest among them is the Zhuang, with a population of over 17 million. Then one may want to know more about the lives and cultures of the minorities, which are so rich and colorful. As China is such a vast nation with so many ethnic groups, it is not easy for an ordinary Chinese to know every minority ethnic group, especially those distributed in remote areas of the country, which seem to be quite mysterious.

However, I believe people who have got some knowledge about the ethnic minorities in China would be attracted by them, even if just for the charms of their wonderful costumes, languages and music. It is with these ethnic minorities that Chinese culture is so prosperous. For outsiders, almost every ethnic minority and the area it inhabits constitute a small world quite different from the mainstream of Chinese society.

Some ethnic minority areas are still little known to the outside world due to their peculiar geographic locations. For instance, in Medog of Tibet Autonomous Region, there live the people of Monba and Lhoba, two ethnic minorities that other people are unfamiliar with. Monba and Lhoba people live among tropical forests in one part of the Tibetan Plateau, keeping their ways of life and customs that have changed little for decades or even a century. Medog was the last county in China to be connected by highway, and it was in the 1980s that it was linked to the outside world. But such a situation is rapidly changing. For a long period of time no particular interest was paid to the rich ethnic cultural resources in the western region, where 70% of China's ethnic minority people live. Today more and more people are visiting the region, attracted by its ethnic minority cultures and extraordinary landscape.

With a brief review of the history of the People's Republic of China since its founding in 1949, we can see that great changes have been taking place in the ethnic groups, including their economic and social conditions, culture and education, folk customs, and values. The demographic distribution of the ethnic minorities has also extended far beyond their traditional areas. Ethnic minority people are found in nearly all cities, and the minority population in urban areas totals over 6 million, or 6.6% of the total population of ethnic minorities. In many ethnic minority areas, while elderlies still speak their native languages, which are almost illegible to outsiders, and sing ancient folksongs, youngsters now know it is necessary for them to study English well, and they show a keen interest in the Internet.... The ethnic minorities in present-day China have integrated many modern elements in their daily lives, but they still preserve their rich cultures and folkways. In this sense, we can say that to know about the ethnic minorities constitutes an important part of one's understanding of China, and that only by learning about their conditions can one understand the success of the ethnic affairs policy of the Chinese government in the past 50 years and more.

POPULATION AND DISTRIBUTION

CHINA

China is a multiethnic nation, with 56 officially identified ethnic groups. Among them the largest is the Han, accounting for over 90% of China's total population, and the 55 others are known as ethnic minorities for their much smaller populations. All the ethnic groups have a long history, but due to evolution they used to have many offshoots and names. As a result, only half a century ago no one could tell the exact number of ethnic groups in China.

Beginning in 1950, the government organized tens of thousands of researchers and workers to carry out a large-scale investigation of the ethnic minorities, including their social history, economic life, folk customs, languages, and religions. The work lasted over a decade. Such an investigation that took huge human, material and financial resources was unprecedented in China, which was in national reconstruction after many years of war and still economically backward, and it was also an endeavor rarely seen in other countries with multiple ethnic groups.

As the investigation went on, the identification of ethnic groups also made progress. In the first national census in 1953, over 400 names of ethnic groups were registered. Careful Studies of their names, origins, distribution, languages, economic life and social history helped to identify 38 minority ethnic groups in 1954. By 1964 another 15 minority ethnic groups were recognized. In 1965 the Lhoba ethnic group was identified. In 1979 the Jino was recognized as a single minority ethnic group. By then the identification of ethnic groups was basically completed in China.

Uygur youngsters in Xinjiang.

After that, apart from investigations to identify a small number of ethnic bodies, efforts were mainly devoted to restoring or altering the ethnic status of a number of ethnic minority people in certain areas, and to classify the identification of certain ethnic bodies.

According to the fifth national census in 2000, the 55 minority ethnic groups in China rank as follows in descending order in terms of the size of population: Zhuang, Manchu, Hui, Miao, Uygur, Tujia, Yi, Mongolian, Tibetan, Bouyei, Dong, Yao, Korean, Bai, Hani, Kazak, Li, Dai, She, Lisu, Gelao, Dongxiang, Lahu, Sui, Va, Naxi, Qiang, Tu, Mulam, Xibe, Kirgiz, Daur, Jingpo, Maonan, Salar, Blang, Tajik, Achang, Primi, Ewenki, Nu, Gin, Jino, De'ang, Bonan, Russian, Yugur, Uzbek, Monba, Oroqen, Derung, Tatar, Hezhen, Gaoshan, Lhoba.

In China, the ethnic status of a citizen is determined either by that of the citizen's father or mother. The ethnic status of a child born or adopted by parents of different ethnic backgrounds is determined by the parents before the child reaches 18 years of age. When the child reaches 18, he or she may choose to determine his/her own ethnic status. No alteration will be made in their ethnic status after such children reach 20 years of age. For remarried couples of different ethnic groups, their children under 18 from the previous marriage will have their ethnic status determined by their parent or stepparent, but children at or over 18 from previous marriage will not alter their ethnic status. Adults will not change their ethnic status due to adoption or marriage. The determined ethnic status of a citizen cannot be altered at discretion.

Population Size

China conducted its fifth national census on November 1, 2000. The census found the nation's population at 1265.83 million (the

Elderly Hui men in front of a mosque in Ningxia. The Hui is the most widely distributed ethnic minority in China, while Ningxia Hui Autonomous Region is the largest Hui community in the country.

Populations of the 56 Ethnic Groups (2000)

Ethnic Group	Pop.(,000 persons)	Ethnic Group	Pop.(,000 persons)
Han	1,159,400	Tu	241.2
Zhuang	16,178.8	Mulam	207.4
Manchu	10,682.3	Xibe	188.8
Hui	9,816.8	Kirgiz	160.8
Miao	8,940.1	Daur	132.4
Uygur	8,399.4	Jingpo	132.1
Tujia	8,028.1	Maonan	107.2
Yi	7,762.3	Salar	104.5
Mongolian	5,813.9	Blang	91.9
Tibetan	5,416.0	Tajik	41.0
Bouyei	2,971.5	Achang	33.9
Dong	2,960.3	Primi	33.6
Yao	2,637.4	Ewenki	30.5
Korean	1,923.8	Nu	28.8
Bai	1,858.1	Gin	22.5
Hani	1,439.7	Jino	20.9
Kazak	1,250.5	De'ang	17.9
Li	1,247.8	Bonan	16.5
Dai	1,159.0	Russian	15.6
She	709.6	Yugur	13.7
Lisu	634.9	Uzbek	12.4
Gelao	579.4	Monba	8.9
Dongxiang	513.8	Oroqen	8.2
Lahu	453.7	Derung	7.4
Sui	406.9	Tatar	4.9
Va	396.6	Hezhen	4.6
Naxi	308.8	Gaoshan	4.5
Qiang	306.1	Lhoba	3.0

populations of Hong Kong, Macao and Taiwan were not included). The Han population was 1159.4 million, or 91.59% of the national total, and the population of the 55 minorities amounted to 106.43 million, or 8.41% of the national total.

Compared with the findings in the fourth national census conducted in 1990, the ethnic minority population increased by 15. 23 million or 15.37%, or 5.48 percentage points more than the increase in the Han population. Most ethnic minority populations rose by a big margin. The populations of Gaoshan, Qiang, Maonan, Bonan and Tujia rose by over 40%, and only a few ethnic minorities had zero or negative growth in population. For instance, the Korean population of over 1.9 million increased by only more than 480 in the decade, the Uzbek population decreased by about 2,300, and the Tatar, by over 170.

Before 1949, many ethnic minorities were suffering from population decrease, and some were even on the verge of ethnic extinction. For instance, in the mid- and late-17th century, the Hezhens had a population of over 12,000, but it dropped to merely more than 300 by 1950. The tragedy came as a result of social and economic backwardness, disasters, wars, poverty, and diseases. At that time ethnic minorities had a low fertility rate and high mortality rate. A popular saying described the situation as "Many pregnant mothers but few walking babies." Since the founding of the People's Republic of China, the government has extended substantial support to ethnic minorities in their economic and cultural development. Thanks to economic growth and improvement in living standards, the mortality rate of the population especially the newly born dropped greatly, and life expectancy increased. In the meantime the government had a much flexible family planning policy for ethnic minorities. Thanks to all this, the trend of population decrease was checked, and the ethnic minority populations boomed.

Sui women, carrying their children on their backs, go to a country fair in Guizhou.

Population Policy

China's population was 541.67 million in 1949, and it rose to 892.11 million in 1973.

As the rapid increase in population exerted great pressure on economic and social development, the government began promoting family planning. In 1981, the Chinese government declared for the first time, "China's population policy is to control the size and raise the quality of the population." The policy calls for late marriage, late and fewer births, and better prenatal care; and it encourages couples to have only one child. In September 1982, family planning was listed as a basic national policy.

In 2002 China enacted the Population and Family Planning Law, which went into force on September 1 the same year. Article 18 of the law provides, "The State keeps its existing family planning policy stable, encourages citizens to practice late marriage and late birth, and encourages couples to have only one child. Couples that meet the requirements of relevant law and regulations may ask for permission to have a second child." This Article also stipulates, "Ethnic minorities shall also practice family planning."

In the past half a century, China's population policy for ethnic minorities has undergone major changes in three periods.

In the first period (1950s-1970s), the government encouraged population growth. Such a policy was adopted to promote the growth and check the decrease in the populations of ethnic minorities.

In the second period (1971-1981), the government reviewed its policy and considered the option of practicing family planning among ethnic minorities. Such a change was made due to the population boom that began in the mid-1960s, which exerted population pressures on some ethnic minority areas.

In the third period (1982 - present), the government decided that ethnic minorities should also practice family planning. In 1982, the Chinese government decided: Family planning should be promoted among ethnic minorities. The policy may have some flexibility, and governments of ethnic autonomous areas and relevant provinces, autonomous regions and municipalities will formulate specific requirements in the light of local conditions, to be enforced after approval by the next higher level of government.

As China's ethnic minorities are widely distributed in areas at different levels of economic, social and cultural development, local governments have formulated different requirements for family planning. The requirements may be classified into three groups.

One. The five autonomous regions, and the provinces of Yunnan, Guizhou and Qinghai, which have a large proportion of ethnic minority population

The policy in Inner Mongolia Autonomous Region allows a couple of the Mongolian ethnic group to have two children, and Mongolian couples not registered in urban areas may have a third child with permission. In this Region, Daur, Ewenki and Oroqen couples are encouraged to have fewer births with better prenatal care; if they ask for birth control service, such service should be provided. Couples of other ethnic groups rather than the Mongolian, Daur, Ewenki and Oroqen are allowed to have at most two children.

The policy of Xinjiang Uygur Autonomous Region allows couples of ethnic minorities in urban areas to have two children and such couples in agricultural or pastoral areas to have three children. The policy also allows the above-mentioned couples to have an additional child in some particular conditions.

In Guangxi Zhuang Autonomous Region, if both husband and wife are of the ethnic minorities of Yao, Miao, Dong, Mulam, Maonan, Hui, Gin, Yi, Sui or Gelao, which each have a population of less than 10 million, a couple may have a second child with

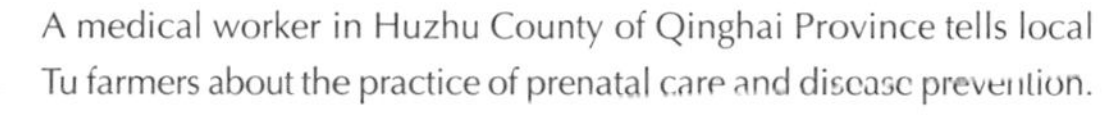

A medical worker in Huzhu County of Qinghai Province tells local Tu farmers about the practice of prenatal care and disease prevention.

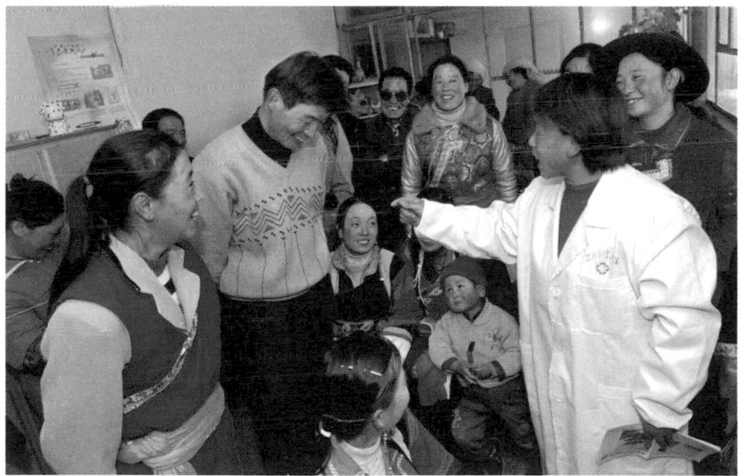

permission.

In Ningxia Hui Autonomous Region, if husband and wife are of ethnic minorities or one of them is of a minority ethnic group, a couple is allowed to have two children. In some mountainous counties farmer couples of ethnic minorities may be allowed to have three children.

In Tibet Autonomous Region, couples of the Tibetan and other minority ethnic groups in urban areas are encouraged to have no more than two children. In agricultural and pastoral areas, couples of ethnic minorities are encouraged to practice late marriage and late birth and have better prenatal care, but they are not subject to any limit of births; if a couple chooses to have family planning, technical guidance will be provided.

In the provinces of Yunnan, Guizhou and Qinghai, the policy is roughly as follows: couples of ethnic minorities are allowed to have two children, and some in agricultural or pastoral areas may have an additional child with permission. But no limit of births is applied to couples of ethnic minorities that have very small populations.

Two. The provinces of Jilin, Liaoning, Heilongjiang, Hebei, Zhejiang, Hubei, Hunan, Guangdong, Hainan, Sichuan and Gansu

These provinces have either autonomous prefectures or autonomous counties with compact communities of ethnic minorities. There couples of minorities are allowed to have two children. In Jilin, a couple of minorities or with husband or wife of a minority is allowed to have two children. In Zhejiang, if both husband and wife are of a minority/minorities, a couple may have a second child with permission; if both husband and wife are farmers or fishermen and one of them is of an ethnic minority, a couple may have a second child with permission.

Three. The municipalities of Beijing, Tianjin and Shanghai, and the provinces of Shanxi, Jiangsu, Anhui, Fujian, Jiangxi, Shandong,

A Tibetan community in Qinghai Province.

Henan and Shaanxi

In these provinces and municipalities, people of ethnic minorities are sparsely distributed. In their population policies the special conditions of ethnic minorities have been taken into consideration. In the three municipalities of Beijing, Tianjin and Shanghai, couples of ethnic minorities are allowed to have two children if they meet certain requirements. In other provinces a couple is allowed to have a second child if both husband and wife are of a minority/minorities.

With years of publicity efforts, people of ethnic minorities have had greater awareness of the family planning policy, and they are willing to observe the policy requirements. In the meantime, the traditional concepts of "carrying on the ancestral line" and "the more children the happier life" have also changed as time passes. Especially in urban areas, as people of younger generations pay more attention to the quality of life, many young couples choose to have only one

A Dong village in Guizhou. The province has many ethnic minorities.

child, for whom they can give better care.

But in rural and especially remote areas the conditions are different. Due to economic and cultural backwardness and influence of traditional ideas, people tend to desire more children especially sons out of the consideration of rearing children against old age. This is because the lack of social security in many areas. Other people may also want to have more children so that their families may have more hands. However, most families have realized that excessive births will have negative impacts and heavier burdens on society, families and individuals; therefore they are willing to observe the government's family planning policy.

Population Distribution

China's ethnic minorities are mainly distributed in the western part of the country, including the provinces and autonomous regions of Guangxi, Yunnan, Guizhou, Xinjiang, Inner Mongolia, Sichuan, Tibet, Qinghai, Gansu, and Ningxia. In 2000 the 12 provinces and autonomous regions in the western region accounted for 28% of the national population but 72% of the nation's population of ethnic minorities. Liaoning Province in the eastern part and Hunan Province in the central part of the country also have quite a large share of minority population. Among all the provinces, autonomous regions and municipalities in China, Guangxi has the biggest minority population (17.21 million), while Tibet has the largest ratio of minority population (94.1%).

Although ethnic minorities account for only a small portion of the national population, they are widely distributed in the country. Ethnic minority people are found in all provinces, autonomous regions and municipalities, and most of the counties have residents of at least two minority ethnic groups. In 2000 the combined population of ethnic minorities accounted for 8.41% of the national

Autumn in Altay, northern Xinjiang. Ethnic minorities account for about 60% of the total population of Xinjiang.

total population. The geographic distribution of China's ethnic groups is not clear-cut but mixed, with compact communities of various ethnic groups mingling each other. In Tibet Autonomous Region, the ethnic minorities account for over 94% of the regional population. In Xinjiang Uygur Autonomous Region, the Han people account for about 40% of the regional population, next only to the Uygur in population size. In the three autonomous regions of Inner Mongolia, Guangxi and Ningxia, the Han population is even larger than that of ethnic minorities. Such a pattern of population distribution has resulted from exchanges between ethnic groups and their migration.

Minority Populations of Provinces, Autonomous Regions and Municipalities

Area	Minority Pop. (,000 persons)	% of Total Pop.	Area	Minority Pop. (,000 persons)	% of Total Pop.
Guangxi	17,210	38.34	Heilongjiang	1,850	5.02
Yunnan	14,330	33.41	Hainan	1,360	17.29
Guizhou	13,340	37.85	Guangdong	1,230	1.42
Xinjiang	11,430	59.39	Henan	1,130	1.22
Liaoning	6,780	16.02	Shandong	620	0.68
Hunan	6,580	10.21	Beijing	590	4.26
Inner Mongolia	4,930	20.76	Fujian	580	1.67
Sichuan	4,150	4.98	Zhejiang	400	0.85
Hebei	2,910	4.31	Anhui	380	0.63
Hubei	2,620	4.34	Tianjin	260	2.64
Jilin	2,460	9.03	Jiangsu	250	0.33
Tibet	2,460	94.07	Shaanxi	180	0.49
Qinghai	2,360	45.51	Jiangxi	110	0.27
Gansu	2,230	8.69	Shanxi	100	0.29
Chongqing	1,980	6.42	Shanghai	100	0.60
Ningxia	1,940	34.53			

Nomadic peoples in China are mostly distributed in the northern and northwestern parts of the country. Now most of them have settled down.

Areas with compact communities of ethnic minorities are usually sparsely populated, in sharp contrast with the populous coastal areas. The population density is about two persons per sq km in Tibet and less than 10 persons per sq km in Qinghai and Xinjiang, compared with 500 to 600 per sq km in eastern Jiangsu and Shandong provinces.

Due to historical reasons, China's ethnic minorities live mostly in frontier areas. Along China's 21,000 km land frontiers are mostly areas inhabited by ethnic minorities. Of all the minority ethnic groups in China, more than 30 live in border areas facing their foreign neighbors of the same ethnic origin. Many border ports have become important trade channels between China and neighboring countries.

The ethnic minority areas are mostly remote, but they enjoy very rich natural, cultural and humanities resources. China's pastoral areas cover about one third of its land territory, and about 94% of the pastures are located in ethnic minority areas, mainly in Inner

Mongolia, Xinjiang, Sichuan, and Tibet. The ethnic minority areas are also the sources of many large rivers in the country, and they account for about one half of the national total of waterpower resources. These areas also claim half of China's forest resources, and three of the four major forest areas in the country. Therefore, many people of the minority ethnic groups used to live on pasturing, fishing and hunting.

These areas also boast rich mineral resources. For instance, Xinjiang accounts for at least one third of China's oil and natural gas reserves, while Inner Mongolia has rich resources of forest in the east, iron ore in the west, grain production in the south and animal husbandry in the north, and other mineral resources in all parts of the region. Inner Mongolia is well known for its cashmere, coal, rare earth and natural gas resources. The key state projects of west-to-east natural gas and electric power transmission started in the early 21st century will transmit energy resources from the ethnic minority people-inhabited western region to the eastern part of the country.

China's ethnic minority people live mostly in mountain areas, highlands, pastoral areas or forest areas, where the landscapes are beautiful and traditional ways of life are preserved. When transport and communication facilities are quite developed today, the environment, life styles, cultures, customs and religions of minority ethnic groups are still very attractive to other people in China. Tibet in the eyes of many people is the most mysterious land free of care, and in the border area between Yunnan, Tibet and Sichuan is Shangri-La, an imaginary paradise on earth that people have long been searching for. The Old Town of Lijiang and the Three Parallel Rivers in Yunnan and the Potala Palace in Tibet have been inscribed on the World Heritage List of the United Nations Educational, Scientific and Cultural Organization. Sites of similar beauty and charms are

Gin fishermen in Guangxi. The Gins are the only ethnic minority people in China that reside by the sea.

many in the areas inhabited by ethnic minorities in China.

Population Migration

The distribution of ethnic minority people has further extended with rapid population migration in China in the past several decades, especially since the 1990s. It was found in the fifth national census conducted in 2000 that ethnic minorities were distributed in the 31 provinces, autonomous regions and municipalities on the mainland, and that 11 of them had people from all the 56 ethnic groups, compared with only one – Beijing – in the fourth national census in 1990.

The fifth national census also found that there was a remarkable flow of ethnic minority people to big cities and the economically developed southeastern coastal region. In the 1990-2000 period, Guangxi Zhuang Autonomous Region, which has the largest ethnic minority population among China's provinces, recorded only a 3.

82% increase in its population of ethnic minorities, while neighboring Guangdong Province saw a 246% increase in its ethnic minority population thanks to a large in-flow of migrant workers and businessmen. In the same period, Zhejiang, Jiangsu and Shanghai also saw their ethnic minority populations rise by at least 50%. Naturally, as the ethnic minority population base in the eastern provinces and municipalities was small, the big-margin increases did not result in a big expansion in absolute terms.

In the ten years since 1990, the share of ethnic minorities in the total population dropped by 3% in Xinjiang, 2% in Tibet, and 0.9% in Guangxi, all ethnic autonomous regions.

Tibet is the largest community of Tibetans in China. In recent years some foreign media reported that the Chinese government launched "large-scale emigration to Tibet," and "Tibetans are becoming an ethnic minority in the Tibetan capital of Lhasa." These reports are however groundless.

According to the latest statistics available from the fifth national census, the population of Tibet Autonomous Region totaled 2,616, 300. Among the total population Tibetans accounted for 2,411,100 or 92.2%; Han people, 155,300 or 5.9%, people of other ethnic minorities, 49,900 or 1.9%.

During China's first national census in 1953, the then Tibetan local government reported that the total population of Tibet was one million. It was found during the second national census in 1964, the third national census in 1982 and the fourth national census in 1990 that Tibetans accounted respectively for 96.6%, 94.4% and 95.5%, and Han people, 2.93%, 4.85% and 3.7%.

The slight decrease in the share of Tibetans in the total population of Tibet is attributed to the demographic standards used in the fifth national census, which took zero hour of November 1, 2000 as the standard time, and the polling covered "people who flowed in but

Tibetan women in traditional costumes on their way to a Lamasery in Lhasa, capital of Tibet Autonomous Region.

not those who flowed out." This means that the statistics included migrant workers and businessmen from other parts of the country who had been in Tibet for half a year or longer, but not Tibetans who went to study or work in other parts of the country.

Many of the Han people in Lhasa and other towns of Tibet are migrants. Every year they come to Tibet in spring to do business in catering or garments or other trades. When winter comes, many of them would go back to their hometowns due to the bitter cold and alpine conditions. As for other people who come to Tibet, many are government officials and professionals who are selected and sent to Tibet to promote the development of Tibet in a continuous supporting-Tibet program. These officials and professionals would work in their own lines for a certain period and then return to their hometowns, replaced by new comers.

REGIONAL AUTONOMY FOR ETHNIC MINORITIES

Regional autonomy for ethnic minorities is a basic political system of China for ethnic affairs. In this system, regional autonomy for ethnic minorities is practiced under the leadership of the central government in areas where people of ethnic minorities live in compact communities, and organs for self-government are established to exercise autonomy.

China has adopted regional autonomy for ethnic minorities out of three considerations.

First, as China has long been a unitary nation under central leadership since ancient times, it conforms to China's national conditions and historical traditions to practice regional autonomy for ethnic minorities.

Second, the mixed geographical distribution of ethnic groups decides that many ethnic minorities live in more than one compact community. The Han people have always constituted the great majority of the Chinese population, while the minority ethnic groups account for only a small percentage. In the early days of the People's Republic of China, the ethnic minorities accounted for only 6% of the national population. Except for Tibet and Xinjiang, in most ethnic minority areas the population of ethnic minorities is smaller than that of the Han ethnic group. Due to their long economic and cultural ties, the ethnic groups are deemed to benefit from cooperation and mutual assistance rather than suffer from separation.

Third, since the Opium War of 1840, various ethnic groups in China had long been working for the common task of fighting against

A ceremony of raising the national flag of China in the square in front of the Potala Palace in Lhasa.

foreign aggression, overthrowing the domestic reactionary rule, and winning national liberation. In such a course they have formed the political consensus of interdependence between the Han and the minority ethnic groups and among the ethnic minorities themselves. This has laid the political and social foundation for a unitary New China with regional autonomy in areas inhabited by ethnic minorities.

In 1984, China enacted the Law on Regional Autonomy for Ethnic Minorities, providing for the rights and duties of self-government in the ethnic autonomous areas in the political, economic and cultural fields. To adapt to new changes, in 2001 the Standing Committee of the National People's Congress enacted amendments to the law. The amendments include new provisions on increasing input in ethnic autonomous areas to step up their development, which were adopted to meet the demands of ethnic minorities and ethnic minority areas for faster economic and social development and to solve their problems. The amendments include mainly provisions on economic and social development, they call for organs of state power at higher levels to assist the ethnic autonomous areas in speeding up development, and they also require economically developed areas to support ethnic autonomous areas as their counterparts designated by the central government.

The Establishment of Ethnic Autonomous Areas

There are five provincial level ethnic autonomous regions in China: Inner Mongolia Autonomous Region, Xinjiang Uygur Autonomous Region, Tibet Autonomous Region, Ningxia Hui Autonomous Region, and Guangxi Zhuang Autonomous Region.

They occupy about 45% of the total land area of China.

The first autonomous region – Inner Mongolia was established in 1947. At that time the autonomous region was much smaller. It did not have its present size until 1956, when other areas were successively incorporated into the region. Situated in northern China, Inner Mongolia covers an area of 1,183,000 sq km, or 12.3% of the country's total land area. In the fifth national census in 2000 the region's population was recorded at 23.76 million, with about one fifth or 4.93 million being of ethnic minorities. The autonomous region has the largest Mongolian community in China, and other smaller compact communities of ethnic minorities include the Manchu, Hui, Daur, Korean, Ewenki and Oroqen.

In 1952, the Central People's Government enacted the Program of the People's Republic of China for the Implementation of Regional Autonomy for Ethnic Minorities, and its implementation began throughout the country.

In Xinjiang, regional autonomy for ethnic minorities was begun first for smaller minority ethnic groups. Located in northwestern China, Xinjiang is the largest provincial administration in China, covering over 1.66 million sq km or about one sixth of the country's land area. In 1954, autonomous prefectures or autonomous counties were established for the Kazak, Mongolian, Hui, Kirgiz, Xibe and Tajik ethnic groups. In 1955, the provincial Xinjiang Uygur Autonomous Region was set up. The fifth national census in 2000 found Xinjiang had a total population of 19.25 million, with 11.43 million being people of minority ethnic groups.

The central government approved the establishment of Guangxi Zhuang Autonomous Region in 1958. Located in southern China, Guangxi covers a land area of 236,000 sq km, or 2.46% of China's total land area. Guangxi ranks the ninth in terms of area among China's provincial divisions. In the fifth national census in 2000 the region's population was recorded at 44.89 million, with 17.21 million being of ethnic minorities.

Urumqi, capital of Xinjiang Uygur Autonomous Region.

In the 1950s, the Hui ethnic group was the third largest in terms of population among China's ethnic minorities, following the Zhuang and Uygur. As the Hui people were scattered throughout the country in some small compact communities, the central government established four autonomous prefectures and a number of autonomous counties for them. In 1958, based on these autonomous areas, the provincial-level Ningxia Hui Autonomous Region was set up. Located in the upper reaches of the Yellow River in western China, this autonomous region covers an area of 66,400 sq km, ranking among the few smallest provincial divisions in the country. The fifth national census in 2000 registered the total population of Ningxia at 5.62 million, with 1.94 million ethnic minority people.

Tibet Autonomous Region was set up in 1965, the last among the five autonomous regions in China. Situated in southwestern China, the region covers over 1.2 million sq km or about 12.8% of China's land area. It is the second largest provincial division next only to Xinjiang. The fifth national census found Tibet's total population at 2.62 million, with 2.41 million Tibetans, accounting for 92% of the total.

While the autonomous regions were established, a large number of autonomous prefectures and autonomous counties (banners – a banner is an administrative division of county level in Inner Mongolia Autonomous Region) were also set up successively in various parts of the country. The establishment of autonomous prefectures or autonomous counties (banners) were usually decided by provincial or autonomous regional governments and reported to the State Council for approval. By 1990, the work of establishing autonomous areas for ethnic minorities was basically completed.

By 2003, there were 155 autonomous areas for ethnic minorities in China, including 5 autonomous regions, 30 autonomous prefectures, and 120 autonomous counties (banners). Of the 55

Hui residents in Beijing cast their ballots to elect deputies to the local people's congress.

minority ethnic groups, 44 have their own autonomous areas, and regional autonomy covers about 71% of the total population of ethnic minorities and 64% of China's land territory.

Types of Autonomous Areas for Ethnic Minorities

Autonomous areas for ethnic minorities in China are of three levels: the autonomous region, autonomous prefecture, and autonomous county (banner). The autonomous areas can also be divided into the following types: 1. Autonomous areas based on the compact community of one minority ethnic group, such as Xinjiang Uygur Autonomous Region. 2. Autonomous areas based on compact communities of two minority ethnic groups, such as Haixi Mongolian and Tibetan Autonomous Prefecture in Qinghai Province. 3.

Autonomous areas based on compact communities of several minority ethnic groups, such as Longsheng Ethnic Autonomous County in Guangxi. 4. Autonomous areas of smaller ethnic minorities within a larger autonomous area, such as Gongcheng Yao Autonomous County in Guangxi Zhuang Autonomous Region. 5. A number of autonomous areas for one ethnic minority whose compact communities are scattered in various parts of the country, such as Ningxia Hui Autonomous Region, Linxia Hui Autonomous Prefecture in Gansu Province, and Dachang Hui Autonomous County in Hebei Province. In some areas with very small compact communities of ethnic minorities that are not qualified for establishment of autonomous areas, ethnic minority townships (towns) are set up.

In China, regional autonomy is not limited to areas where the ethnic minority population constitutes the majority; it may be practiced by minority ethnic groups of either large or small population size. Autonomous areas for ethnic minorities usually cover some communities of the Han people, and in quite a few of the areas the Han population is even larger than that of ethnic minorities.

Due to their different patterns of population distribution, ethnic minorities may have more than one autonomous area. Some ethnic minorities such as the Mongolian, Hui, Tibetan and Zhuang have their own autonomous regions, but they also have one or several autonomous prefectures or autonomous counties or share such prefectures or counties with other minority ethnic groups in other parts of the country. The Uygur people however only have Xinjiang Uygur Autonomous Region but not other autonomous areas. Some ethnic minorities such as the Miao and Tujia have their own autonomous prefectures in one place and also other autonomous prefectures or counties in other places, or share such autonomous areas with other ethnic minorities. Some ethnic minorities such as the Kirgiz have only one autonomous prefecture. Some ethnic minorities have established a number of autonomous counties in several provinces. For instance, the Manchu has 12 autonomous counties either of its own or shared with other ethnic minorities. Other ethnic minorities including the Oroqen and Ewenki each have only one autonomous county.

The Composition of Organs of Self-Government for Ethnic Minorities

Organs of self-government in ethnic autonomous areas refer to the people's congresses and people's governments of autonomous regions, autonomous prefectures and autonomous counties.

Organs of self-government in ethnic autonomous areas are local organs of state power under the unified leadership of the central government. They are the same as ordinary local organs of state power in creation, terms of office, institution and principles of performance. The people's congress of an ethnic autonomous area exercises the powers of legislation, making decisions on major issues, selection and appointment of personnel, and supervision. The permanent organ of a people's congress is its standing committee. The government of an ethnic autonomous area is the executive organ of the people's congress, and the chief executive shoulders the overall responsibility. On the basis of democratic deliberation, the chief executives of governments at various levels are empowered to make final decisions on major issues in their governments, and take full responsibility for the decisions and the work in their jurisdictions.

The chief executives of the organs of self-government in ethnic autonomous areas are selected from among the minority ethnic groups that exercise regional autonomy in the respective areas, a practice different from that for organs of state power in other areas.

For instance, since the establishment of Tibet Autonomous Region in 1965, all the chairmen of the standing committee of regional people's congress and regional government have been people of Tibetan ethnicity. Statistics show that the region has now over 50, 000 officials with minority ethnic backgrounds, and that Tibetans account for over 70% of all officials in the region.

The law provides that the composition of the organs of self-government of regional autonomy for ethnic minorities must meet the following requirements:

1. The people's congress of an ethnic autonomous area shall include both deputies from among the ethnic group (or groups) that exercises regional autonomy and a certain number of deputies from among people of other ethnic groups that reside in the area. Among the chairman and vice-chairmen of the standing committee of the people's congress of an ethnic autonomous area there shall be one or more citizens of the minority ethnic group (or groups) that exercises regional autonomy.

2. The chairman of an autonomous region, the prefect (commissioner) of an autonomous prefecture or the head of an autonomous county shall be a citizen of the ethnic group/groups that exercises regional autonomy in the area concerned. The people's governments of such areas shall apply the system of giving overall responsibility to the chairman of an autonomous region, the prefect of an autonomous prefecture or the head of an autonomous county, who shall direct the work of the governments at their respective levels.

3. The other members of the government in an ethnic autonomous area should, whenever possible, be chosen from citizens of the ethnic group/groups exercising regional autonomy and of the other minority ethnic groups in the area.

Performance at an ethnic minorities arts festival.

The Power of Autonomy of the Organs of Self-Government in Ethnic Autonomous Areas

Self-government is naturally somewhat different from governments in other areas. Take Tibet Autonomous Region for instance.

Tibet as an autonomous region enjoys both the legislative power of a local administrative division, that is, to enact local rules and regulations, and the power of self-government as stipulated by the law on ethnic regional autonomy. While observing the national Constitution, the autonomous region is empowered to enforce relevant national laws and regulations with certain alterations in the light of local conditions. Since 1965 Tibet has enacted over 150 local rules, regulations, decisions and resolutions, which have all taken local conditions into consideration.

For instance, apart from the national legal holidays, the region's legal holidays also include traditional Tibetan holidays such as the

Deputies of ethnic minorities attending a session of the National People's Congress in Beijing.

New Year of the Tibetan Calendar and the Xodoin festival. In the light of local natural conditions, the regional government set the weekly working hours for employees at 35, five hours less than the national legal working hours of a week.

In 1981, Tibet enacted the Rules on Alterations in the Enforcement of the Marriage Law of the People's Republic of China in Tibet Autonomous Region. Historically both polyandry and polygamy were allowed in Tibet. The regional Rules uphold the basic principles of the Marriage Law, that is, freedom of marriage and monogamy, and nullify the outdated marriage system of polyandry and polygamy. However, in the light of Tibet's conditions, the Rules allow the de facto marriage relations of polyandry and polygamy that had been formed before the enactment of the Rules, should the persons involved not voluntarily ask for nullification of the relations. In implementing the Rules, local governments try to persuade people involved in polyandry or polygamy to shift to monogamy, but those who refuse to change are not regarded as offenders of bigamy. To honor the historical customs in Tibet, the legal minimum age limits for marriage in the region are set at 20 years for male and 18 for female, both 2 years younger than the provisions in the national Marriage Law.

In addition, the power of self-government is also found in various aspects of the political, economic, cultural and educational fields and social life. Take the use of language for example.

It is stipulated in Tibet Autonomous Region that both the Tibetan and Chinese languages are used in the region, with Tibetan as the main language. Tibetan is the commonly used language in the region, and both the Tibetan and Chinese languages are used for the resolutions, rules and orders adopted by the people's congress and the official documents and announcements issued by governments at various levels. In judicial practice, the Tibetan language is used for litigants of the Tibetan ethnicity in handling cases and legal documents. The press, radio and television stations in Tibet use both the Tibetan and Chinese languages, and signs of the two languages are applied to institutions, streets, roads and public facilities.

In accordance with the Constitution, the Law on Ethnic Regional Autonomy and other laws, apart from the regular functions of local organs of state power, the organs of self-government in ethnic autonomous areas exercise the power of autonomy in the light of political, economic and cultural conditions of the local minority ethnic groups.

Such power includes the following:

1. Legislation. The people's congresses of ethnic autonomous areas shall have the power to enact regulations on the exercise of autonomy and separate regulations in the light of the political, economic and cultural characteristics of the ethnic minority or minorities in the areas concerned. The regulations on the exercise of autonomy and separate regulations of autonomous regions shall be submitted to the Standing Committee of the National People's Congress for approval before they go into effect. The regulations on the exercise of autonomy and separate regulations of autonomous prefectures and autonomous counties shall be submitted to the standing committees of the people's congresses of provinces or autonomous regions for approval before they go into effect, and they shall be reported to the Standing Committee of the National People's Congress for the record.

2. Administration. If a resolution, decision, order or instruction of a state organ at a higher level does not suit the conditions in an ethnic autonomous area, the organ of self-government of the area may either implement it with certain alterations or cease implementing it after reporting to and receiving the approval of the state organ at a higher level.

3. Economic development. The organ of self-government of an ethnic autonomous area shall have the power to formulate principles, policies and plans for economic development in the light of local

Students from the Central University for Nationalities salute to the national flag in Tiananmen Square in Beijing.

conditions and needs of the ethnic minority or minorities and the areas concerned, and to adjust the relations of production and reform the structure of economic management. With approval from the State Council, ethnic autonomous areas may open foreign trade ports and enjoy certain preferential treatments in foreign trade activities.

4. Finance. The organs of self-government of ethnic autonomous areas shall have the power of autonomy in administering the finances of their areas. All revenues accruing to the ethnic autonomous areas shall be managed and used by the organs of self-government of these areas on their own. If the expenditures of an ethnic autonomous area exceed its revenues, the financial department at a higher level shall grant a subsidy. Ethnic autonomous areas are entitled to special funds

and subsidies allocated by the state. While implementing the tax laws of the state, the organs of self-government of ethnic autonomous areas may grant tax exemptions or reductions for certain items of local financial income, in addition to items on which tax reduction or exemption require unified examination and approval by the state.

5. The organs of self-government of ethnic autonomous areas may, in accordance with the military system of the state and local needs and with the approval of the State Council, organize local public security forces for the maintenance of public order.

6. In accordance with the local needs, the organs of self-government of ethnic autonomous areas shall take various measures to train large numbers of cadres at different levels and various kinds of specialized personnel, including scientists, technicians and managerial executives, as well as skilled workers from among the local ethnic groups, and shall pay attention to the training of cadres at various levels and specialized and technical personnel of various kinds from among the women of ethnic minorities.

7. While performing its functions, the organ of self-government of an ethnic autonomous area shall, in accordance with the regulations on the exercise of autonomy of the area, use one or several languages commonly used in the locality; where several commonly used languages are used for the performance of such functions, the language of the ethnic group exercising regional autonomy may be used as the main language.

8. The organs of self-government of ethnic autonomous areas shall independently develop science, technology, culture and education. They shall independently develop education for ethnic minorities, set up various kinds of schools, decide on the plans for the development of education in these areas, on the establishment of various kinds of schools at different levels, on their educational system, forms, curricula, the language used in instruction and

enrollment procedures. They shall also independently develop literature, art, the press, publishing, radio broadcasting, the film industry, television and other cultural undertakings in forms and with characteristics of the ethnic groups. They shall make independent decisions on local plans for developing science and technology and spreading knowledge of science and technology. They shall make independent decisions on plans for developing local medical and health services and for advancing both modern medicine and the traditional medicine of the ethnic groups. They shall independently develop sports, and promote the traditional sports of the ethnic groups. They shall protect the scenic spots and historical sites in their areas, their precious cultural relics and other important historical and cultural legacies, and develop their fine traditional cultures.

THE ECONOMY AND SOCIETY

Before the 1950s, most of China's minorities engaged in agricultural production, but they were at different levels of development – some engaged in intensive farming, others in extensive farming, and still others, slash-and-burn farming or primitive agriculture. Usually when ethnic minorities lived mingled with or near the Han community, their economic activities were at roughly the same level as the Han people. Such ethnic minorities included the Hui, Zhuang, Manchu and Korean communities. Some ethnic minorities lived on fishing and hunting, supplemented by primitive farming and animal husbandry – among them were the Hezhen, Oroqen, Ewenki, and Gin. Some ethnic minorities were traditionally nomad, such as Kazak, Kirgiz, Tajik, Yugur, and some of the Mongolian and Tibetan people. Some ethnic minorities like the Hui had traditionally engaged in some industrial and commercial operations, especially among Hui people in large and midsize cities were some owners of textile and leather mills. But generally speaking businessmen of ethnic minorities were few. Before 1949, when New China was founded, most of the ethnic minority communities had no modern industry, and some had even not completed the division of labor between animal husbandry and agriculture or between farming and the handicraft industry.

Only half a century has passed, yet the thousand-year-old modes of production of the ethnic minorities have changed greatly. Although most of them still engage in agriculture or animal husbandry, theirs are no longer subsistence economies. In the countryside and on

Tibetan farmers harvesting wheat.

grasslands, there have emerged new villages and towns. Some are running factories, doing commercial activities or working in service industries, and more and more ethnic minority people are working in trades their ancestors have never touched. Such changes are numerous and complicated. It will take volumes to analyze the changes of one ethnic minority or only one of its communities. In this book we will only give some sketches of the changes to our readers.

Out of the Subsistence Economy

Let's first see what has happened in the life of the Kucong people, who were once believed to be a separate ethnic minority.

In the early 1950s, the Kucong people lived in the Ailao Mountain in southwest China's Yunnan Province. They were scattered in virgin forests, with one to five families in one place. Although they grew some corn and dry rice crops, the output from slash-and-burn farming was quite low, and they had to gather fruits and herbs or hunt animals to make up for the grain shortage for three to six months a year. At that time every three Kucong families shared an iron axe, which was obtained through barter trade. They used bows and arrows in hunting, and partitioned large games. Many Kucong people had no clothing, and they covered their bodies with animal skins, leaves or rags. As they had no bowls, they would use banana leaves to hold

A Hani woman and her children in Yuanyang of Yunnan. In the background are terrace fields, which Hani people have been tending for generations.

food.

As they had no permanent fields, they would move wherever they slashed and burned for farming, and most people lived in huts built of bamboo, branches and banana leaves. Some people even stayed under rocks or in tree holes. Some people rubbed bamboo to make fire just as primitives did. In their huts there was an ever-burning fire, and people would sleep on grass or leaves around the fire as they had no quilt. When there was a heavy rain, the whole family would gather around the fire to make sure that it did not extinguish.

The Kucong people had almost no belongings. They obtained the few clothes, matches, salt and ironware they had through exchange. When they wanted to barter something, they would put their animal skins, medicinal herbs or bamboo articles by the roadside near villages of other ethnic groups, and hid nearby till the traders left and then came out to collect the bartered goods. Sometimes when they met with unfair trade or even looting, they would shoot arrows or throw stones in protest. If they did not shoot arrows or throw stones, then that means they agreed to the deal. Such a "mute trading" stopped only after the Kucong people settled down in the late 1950s.

To help the Kucong people move out of forests, the people's government of Jinping County began to try to persuade them to settle down in 1952, when the government was just founded. But it was not easy to find the Kucong people, for they would run away once they saw any strangers. Later, the government organized ethnic affairs work teams to work in the villages of the Hani and Yao ethnic groups. With the help of Hani and Yao people, the work teams sent grain and clothes to Kucong people in the forests time and again. Gradually some Kucong people moved out of virgin forests.

The government built houses for them, provided them with farm tools, farm cattle and other articles for daily use, and built schools for their children. Education and medical care were given to them free of charge. Neighboring people of other ethnic minorities also donated some fields to them and taught them how to farm and live in settlement. However, Kucong people were not used to such a new way of life at first, and some moved back into forests. It was after repeated efforts that the over 2,100 Kucong people finally moved out of forest and settled down in the 1960s.

In the meantime, ethnic identification for the Kucong people was carried out. In 1984, the government of Jinping County organized a Kucong delegation to visit the Lahu people in Lancang Lahu

Autonomous County. The Kucong delegates and Lahu people talked with each other about their languages, folkways and customs, and gave performances of their dances and songs. In this way many common things were discovered. Finally in 1987 the Kucong people were identified as an offshoot of the Lahu ethnic group.

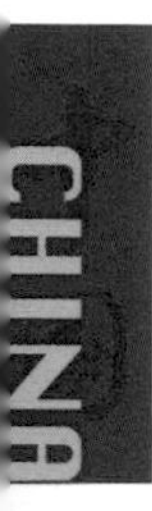

The Kucong people live mostly in Zhemi Township of Jinping County, with a population of over 5,400. The local government had long been providing relief to them. However, Kucong people were still in poverty due to the remoteness of their community, poor transport and communication facilities, and low level of educational attainment, as well as the fact that most Kucong people lacked skills of production and managing money matters. In 1998 the Yunnan provincial government launched a poverty-reduction program for the Kucong people, deciding to spend 10 million yuan a year to help over 5,000 Kucong people get out of poverty in about 5 years. The government also sent ethnic affairs work teams to Kucong villages, and they ran training classes for villagers to learn production techniques and other knowledge, and helped them cultivate awareness of the market economy.

With government funding and local labor, Zhemi Township built roads and water conservation projects and got power supply. Kucong people, who used to have little knowledge of commodities, began their own businesses, such as contracting to run tea plantations, raising animals, and engaging in commercial activities. With just three or four years' efforts, quite a few people have built new houses, six villages have set up satellite ground stations, five villages have installed telephone lines, and over 50 households have bought television sets.

Like the Kucong people, the ethnic minorities in China have realized a fundamental change in their economic development just over half a century, that is, shifting from the natural economy to the

Two Miao girls in traditional costumes at a trade fair in Guizhou. They are selling local farm products.

commodity economy. In 2000, Yunnan University conducted a regional survey of ethnic minorities, which covered 25 villages in Yunnan. The first-hand findings would help us have a better understanding of their economic conditions.

Situated in southwest China, Yunnan has an area of 394,000 sq km, with 370,000 sq km of mountain areas. The province has 25 ethnic minorities each with at least 5,000 people, making it the first among Chinese provinces in terms of the number of ethnic minorities.

Of the 25 villages covered by the survey, 90% are in mountain areas. In terms of economic development, these villages were much better off than the Kucong people, but worse than many other ethnic minority communities in the country. Before the 1980s these villages engaged in merely agricultural production, but now they have also started some industrial and service businesses.

Of all the villages, those in the higher-end segment have one thing in common: they have a tradition of commercial and handicraft activities. For instance, in Nagu Town of Tonghai County in Yuxi City, villagers of the Hui ethnic group have a tradition of making knives. In the early 1980s they made knives by hand in family workshops. With funds thus accumulated, they moved on to making steel window frames, which brought about steel rolling, welding and hardware manufacturing. Today, Nagu has become the largest base of welded tubes and steel window frames in Yunnan, and some producers have an annual output value of over 100 million yuan.

In the villages in the medium segment, people engage mainly in farming. However, they are moving away from the traditional way of farming by using machines and modern techniques, and they are also changing the production pattern by relying more on cash crops and raising animals.

Some villagers still keep to their traditional way of production. For instance, tobacco is a major cash crop in Nagu Town, but none of the Hui villagers grow tobacco. Even when they contract their plots of land to others, they would not allow the contractors to grow tobacco plants on the plots.

In the past, whether they were farmers or craftsmen, villagers lived a subsistence life with little extra revenue. Now service trades have developed in the villages. Some villagers have bought farm vehicles and trucks to engage in transportation. In some villages near tourist attractions people have started catering and retailing businesses. Villagers who have not funds to start their own businesses would usually become migrant workers.

A horizontal comparison would find that these villages still lag behind other areas in economic development, as they are restrained by geographical conditions, lack of technology, and backward ideas. But vertically these villages have made greater progress in the past few decades than in thousands of years in history.

Ewenki women making birch bark articles in the Greater Hinggan Mountains, Inner Mongolia.

Bidding Farewell to the Life on Fishing and Hunting

On January 23, 1996, the government of Oroqen Autonomous Banner in Inner Mongolia, the compact community of the Oroqen ethnic group, issued a notice, banning the hunting, selling, purchasing and transportation of wild animals by any institution or individual, including Oroqen hunters. This marked the end of this ethnic minority's long history of hunting.

Before the 1950s, the Oroqen people lived in virgin forests in the Greater and Lesser Hinggan Mountains in the Northeast. They made a living on hunting, plus collecting and fishing. They moved from place to place, and led a hard life. At that time a foreign researcher asserted after investigating the Oroqens, "This ethnic group that

Manzhouli on the Sino-Russian border is the largest land port in China. The port handles large amounts of imports and exports.

depends on games from the Greater Hinggan Mountains will soon disappear."

In 1951, Oroqen Banner was established. Although the ethnic group had only over 700 people at that time, the banner was made an autonomous banner the next year on the principle of equality for all ethnic groups. The banner was the first county-level ethnic autonomous area in China. The government provided new rifles and bullets for Oroqen hunters to improve their production. In the meantime, the government also encouraged Oroqen people to settle down and end their primitive way of life. Oroqen youngsters were sent to other areas to study, free medical care was provided for the hunters, and every male hunter of Oroqen ethnicity was listed on payroll as a forest guard.

As they used to move from place to place and lived on hunting, the Oroqens at first had some apprehension about settling down. After several years of persuasion and preparation, in 1958 they moved out of forests and settled down in the hunters' villages built with government funds. The government also set up clinics and schools at the villages.

With increase in population and exploitation of forest resources, the number of wild animals in forests dropped year by year, and it became difficult for Oroqens to lead a traditional life on hunting. Many hunters were unwilling to learn other production techniques, and they had to keep subsistence by a few games and the limited government subsidies. In contrast, those who were willing to learn and accept new production means such as farming and raising animals gradually got rich, and they became role models for others.

In such a drastic transformation of the mode of production, the hunters could not simply rely on their own efforts. The local government first built roads to facilitate exchange of goods between towns and villages. The government also installed electric power and telephone lines, and bought television sets for the Oroqen hunters, so that they could get more information from the outside world. Every year the agriculture department would send technicians to Oroqen villages to run training classes and guide villagers in their production. The close environment was thus altered, and the hunters' mentality also changed greatly.

In 1996 the government began imposing hunting prohibition. Naturally hunters were reluctant to put down their guns and shift to a new way of life, but in the end they observed the ban for the sake of protecting forest and animal resources and ecological conservation. To smooth the shift, the local government adopted preferential policy measures. As the ban was in effect, hunters began to get monthly allowances, the government allocated lands to them, and in some places the former hunters were allowed to reclaim as much land as they could. The government also provided loans and subsidies for them.

Now Oroqen people work on both family and collective farms. They grow grain and cash crops and medicinal herbs, make handicraft articles, and engage in tourism operations with their ethnic characteristics.

The Oroqens, who are no longer hunters, now live in brick houses. The five Oroqen townships have set up their own hospitals, and provide free medical care for local residents. Their life expectancy has increased from 45 years to about 60 years, and the total Oroqen population rose from 1,300 to over 3,800. Historically Oroqens practiced intermarriage within the ethnic group. Now that they have settled down, more and more Oroqen young people have married people from other ethnic groups.

Every Oroqen hunters' village has now at least one primary school, and some of the schools have set up multimedia labs and distance education network. This is in sharp contrast with the situation in 1951, when the just established Oroqen Banner had only one primary school. High school students of Oroqen ethnicity are now fully supported by the Banner's finance, and those who are enrolled in institutions of higher learning get bonuses from the government.

Similar to the case of Oroqen people, the Hezhen people are also bidding farewell to a life on fishing and hunting. The Hezhens live in the valleys of the Heilong, Songhua and Wusuli rivers in the Northeast, with a population of over 4,500. The only three Hezhen townships in China are situated in Tongjiang City and the counties of Fuyuan and Raohe of Heilongjiang Province.

For generations the Hezhens lived on fishing and hunting. In the past the Heilong River teemed with fish, and in high fishing season fish themselves would sometimes jump into boats. Now fish resources are rapidly decreasing, and the government has banned fishing in the river – the Hezhens are an exception, they are still allowed to fish in the river due to their tradition.

However, Hezhens who live on fishing are also decreasing. Beginning in the 1990s some Hezhens have lived ashore by growing

A Pasture in the Tianshan Mountains, Xinjiang.

crops and planting trees. In Jiejinkou Hezhen Township of Tongjiang City, many people now engage in the tourism industry. With support from the local government, the township built a Hezhen Folkways Village to attract visitors. The village has a fishing ground, a hunting ground, a Hezhen folkways museum, and an art performance troupe. The peculiar landscape, folkways, food and environment attract tourists from everywhere.

Traditionally the Hezhens took fish for food and fish skin for clothing, therefore they were also known as the "Fish Skin Tribe". In modern times cotton cloth has replaced fish skin. To make a suit of fish skin would take high craftsmanship and two to three months of time. Nowadays the Hezhens would wear their traditional garments only on major holidays or in traditional activities. But the craftsmanship will not be lost, for fish skin garments have become handicraft articles for visitors.

Compared with the Hezhens, the Gin people live a far modern life.

The Gin is the only ethnic minority in China that lives by the sea.

The Gin population totals over 22,000, and nearly half of them live on three islets off Dongxing City in Guangxi. Till the late 1980s the Gins got their income mainly from offshore fishing, but poor transportation made it difficult for them to sell their hard-earned catch. Later, their area was opened as a tourism resort. As the place is far from cities and with no industry, the fine environment and fresh air attract numerous tourists. In high season of tourism, a small shop by the sea would make good money just by renting chairs and selling snacks and drinks.

Gin families usually engage in diversified operations. Since the 1990s border trade, aquatic cultivation, tourism and aquatic products processing have accounted for the largest four sources of income of Gin people. As their ancestors came from Vietnam, the Gin people speak fluent Vietnamese and know the Vietnamese market quite well. Therefore, apart from border trade, many Gin people also work as interpreters or intermediaries.

On the peninsula inhabited by Gin people, a high-level highway has been built, and there are also quite a number of hotels, restaurants, shops, bank offices, and Internet cafes. Ten years ago brick houses and bicycles were commonplace in the area, and now nearly every household has a three-story building, motorcycles and home appliances. Some families have bought cars.

The Gins used to hold grand sacrifice ceremonies before going offshore, praying for safe sailing and big catches. Such ceremonies known as Ha still continue, but they are now for entertainment rather than for sacrifice. At a time when their folk culture faces shocks from modern civilization, the Gins began to pay more attention to protect their cultural heritage. People made donations for maintenance of the Ha Pavilion. Ha means singing in the Gin language. The Ha Pavilion is not only a site for sacrifice, but also a venue for Gin people to meet, sing and chat. Some Gin musicians have enrolled students to teach them to play the traditional Single-Stringed Qin, a peculiar Gin musical instrument. In primary and high schools, the traditional sport of jumping over bamboo rods is listed in physical education.

A pastoral area in Xinjiang.

From Nomad to Settled Life

There are vast grasslands in the provinces and autonomous regions of Inner Mongolia, Xinjiang, Tibet, Gansu and Qinghai in the northern and western parts of China. For a long time, many people there, mostly of the Mongolian, Tibetan, Kazak, Kirgiz, Yugur and Tajik ethnic groups, lived a nomad life.

These people moved according to the seasons from place to place in search of food, water, and grazing land. This mode of pasturing results in low and unstable yields, for the fertility of animals is low and their resistance to disasters is weak. For instance, in 1977 a blizzard destroyed 90% of the livestock in Xilin Gol League in Inner Mongolia. In the meantime, life was indeed very hard for the families of herdsmen, as they had to move with the animals, sometimes several hundred kilometers a year. Their yurts were rather simple, and the families had to sleep on grass. Such a simple life leads to various diseases. As the herdsmen lived sparsely, patients had to travel long distance before reaching a hospital. In the pastoral areas education was also a big problem.

The government began in the 1950s to encourage nomad herdsmen to build fixed homes and to combine pasturing with farming, and also to take animal products processing as a sideline. By the 1980s, pastoral areas had all implemented a contract responsibility system, in which grasslands were partitioned and contracted to households for a fixed period of time. The contractors are responsible to protect and improve the grasslands. This move greatly aroused the enthusiasm of herdsmen, and most of them abandoned nomad life to live in fixed or semi-fixed homes. Many of them are no longer herdsmen in the original sense, for they also grow cash crops while herding cattle and sheep. New villages and towns have appeared in pastoral grounds the herdsmen used to visit.

Since the 1990s, another drastic change has been taking place in the mode of production and lifestyle of herdsmen. As the number of animals increased, overgrazing and droughts led to desertification of grasslands. To protect the ecological environment, the government decided that a shift from pasturing to raising animals in livestock sheds should be made. This means the traditional mode of animal husbandry is changing to achieve both economic and ecological benefits.

According to the government policy, pastoral areas in good conditions are divided for rotating grazing, in areas where pasturing is banned herdsmen are given cash and grain as subsidies, and the government also assists herdsmen to improve grasslands by growing grass and improving animal breeds. The government has helped herdsmen from areas with serious desertification to move to places with good conditions, and encouraged them to change their mode of production. The new settlements were built mainly with government funds, where roads, electricity, postal service, water supply and television broadcast are all available. In these areas, people who engage in businesses other than agriculture and animal husbandry are entitled to preferential tax treatment.

After the livestock are kept in sheds, the typical scene of cattle and sheep roaming on the grasslands is rarely seen, but the grasslands themselves regain their beauty. Grasslands tourism has become a passion, bringing new jobs and more income for local people. In the past, the Mongolians and Kazaks used to be known as nomad tribes. But things have changed greatly. For instance, the Kazaks in Xinjiang depended mainly on animal husbandry till the 1950s. In the 1980s two thirds of the Kazaks had become farmers, and only one third

Grasslands and folkways are major tourism resources in Inner Mongolia.

still engaged in pasturing. In the meantime they have got many new ideas. Historically Kazak communities had no trade in commodities, and Kazaks thought it immoral and infamous to be a trader. Therefore before the 1950s there were few Kazak businessmen. Since the 1990s, as the market economy boomed, many private businessmen have come to Xinjiang, and products of herdsmen have become commodities. As a result quite a few Kazaks have become businessmen: they process and sell animal products and embroidery articles, and they run hotels and restaurants to serve tourists. A formerly nomad ethnic group now engages in animal husbandry, agriculture, industry, and commerce.

Unlike their ancestors who moved from place to place searching for water and pasturing grounds, and riding on the grasslands, herdsmen now live in warm houses, using coal and gas for cooking and owning home appliances, and they also enjoy modern cultural, educational and medical services.

Government Assistance

In the early years of the People's Republic, the economy of the

Winter supplies for Tibetans arrive at Gonggar Airport in Lhasa.

ethnic minorities was rather backward. In 1949 the total industrial and agricultural output value of the areas inhabited by ethnic minorities accounted for only 7.8% of the national total. Since then, the government has taken many policy measures to accelerate economic development in those areas.

One. Preferential policies in finance, taxation, banking, investment and trade

As early as the 1960s the state had adopted three preferential policy measures for ethnic autonomous areas. First, apart from their budget expenditures, an extra of 5% funds was allotted to them; second, they enjoyed much higher fiscal reserves than other areas; and third, a certain amount of subsidies for ethnic minority areas was set each year. Beginning in 1980, the subsidies from the central government to the five autonomous regions and the provinces of Yunnan, Guizhou and Qinghai were increased by 10% a year. These policy measures were in effect till 1988. In that year the subsidies were set at the 1988 level for future years.

In 1994 the central government reformed the taxation system to share tax revenues with localities, but its policy of subsidics and special funds for ethnic autonomous areas remained unchanged. Apart from the regular fiscal subsidies, the central government also provided special financial assistance to such areas, such as funds for education in border areas and ethnic minority areas, for economic development in border areas, for development of underdeveloped areas, and for the development of Tibet.

In taxation, the central government has given more decision-making powers to ethnic autonomous areas. Local governments in other areas have the power to decide exemption or reduction of taxes on slaughtering animals, banquets and agricultural and animal husbandry production, but the provincial-level governments of ethnic autonomous areas have the power to decide exemption or reduction of taxes on any items that go to the local financial revenue. In the meantime, the state also offers appropriate tax exemption or reduction to ethnic autonomous areas, such as those on agricultural production in poverty-stricken areas, enterprises, trading, and production of goods for ethnic minorities.

The policy measures in banking include special loans, preferential interest rates, more credit lines and extension of repayment terms. For instance, the government has set up special loans for ethnic minorities-related trade, and special interest-free loans for poverty reduction in pastoral areas. The government also requires that banking institutions should extend credit support to fixed asset investment projects in ethnic autonomous areas and to enterprises in those areas that conform to the state's industrial policies in exploiting resources and developing diversified operations.

In investment, the state offers preferential treatment to encourage both domestic and foreign capital to invest in ethnic autonomous areas. In accordance with unified planning and market demand, the state gives priority to projects of resources development and infrastructure construction in ethnic autonomous areas. The state puts a bigger share of investment in and allocates more loans from policy banks to major infrastructure projects in these areas.

The state also extends investment, banking and taxation support to commercial, supply and marketing and pharmaceutical enterprises in ethnic autonomous areas. For instance, in the 1960s the state decided to give preferential treatment to commercial enterprises in 159 counties of such areas, which were poverty-stricken, remote and with poor transport facilities. To date the conditions in these counties have greatly improved, but the preferential treatment remains the same, and the number of counties enjoying such treatment has increased to over 400. The preferential treatment includes: favorable interest rates, tax exemption and reduction,

The Qinghai-Tibet Railway now under construction will run over 1,100 km from Golmud in Qinghai to Lhasa, capital of Tibet. The railway is expected to open to traffic in 2007.

special loans, price subsidies for special goods, subsidies for transport expenses of daily use goods in remote and backward areas, supply of special materials, funds for construction of commercial networks and technical upgrading, and stores in cities that sell ethnic minorities-oriented goods.

In foreign trade, the state gives more decision-making power to producers in ethnic autonomous areas, encourages them to expand export of products with comparative advantage by providing preferential treatment to them in planning, quotas and licensing, and enforces preferential policy measures for border trade.

Two. Making favorable arrangements for ethnic minority areas in economic development plans

The state empowers ethnic minority areas to decide on their own economic development. Under the guidance of state plans, the organs of self-government of ethnic autonomous areas shall formulate their own principles, policies and plans for economic development, and independently arrange for and administer local economic development.

To tap the rich resources in ethnic minority areas, in the 1950s to 1960s the state started a number of key projects in Inner Mongolia, Xinjiang, Ningxia, Gansu and Jilin. Among them were the iron and steel complex in Baotou of Inner Mongolia, Qingtongxia hydropower station in Ningxia, Liujiaxia hydropower station in Gansu, oil exploration in Xinjiang, and the development of forest resources in the Hinggan Mountains of Inner Mongolia and Changbai Mountains in the Northeast. Also built in the period were a number of supporting energy and transportation projects. As a result these areas began their own modern industry. By the late 1950s, the state moved a number of industrial enterprises to some ethnic minority areas in the northwest and the southwest, which further accelerated industrial development there. The ethnic minority areas boast rich resources of waterpower, petroleum, natural gas and minerals. In recent years the state has adopted favorable policies for the development of such industries in these areas. The development of energy and mineral resources was stepped up, and relevant manufacturing industries were launched to tap the local advantages.

The state has adopted preferential policies for the development of natural resources in ethnic minority areas. For instance, as stipulated by law and the state's unified planning, organs of self-government of ethnic autonomous areas enjoy priority in developing and using local natural resources. Those ethnic autonomous areas that export their resources get compensation from the state. The coal, electricity and forestry enterprises set up by the central government in ethnic minority areas leave part of their products and profits to the localities to support their economic and cultural development. In exploration and exploitation of mineral resources, the state stipulates that the revenues will be shared by the central and local

The Karamay Oilfield in Xinjiang.

governments: the ratio between the central government and provincial or municipal governments is 5:5, but that between the central government and the autonomous regional governments is 4:6.

Three. Regional development policy for narrowing gaps and common prosperity

Due to natural, historical, social and economic reasons, the areas inhabited by ethnic minorities lag behind the eastern coastal areas, not only in economic development, but also in awareness of the market economy, infrastructure, the markets, and social development.

Since 1978, when China began its reform and opening up, the country's regional development strategy has experienced four stages in the definitions of policy, namely: giving priority to the eastern coastal areas, balanced development of the east and the west, supporting the development of the central and western regions, and implementing the western development strategy. Although the regional development strategy is not exactly the same as the development strategy for ethnic minority areas, the western development strategy formulated in 1999 is closely related to the development of ethnic minority areas, for three fourths of the west is inhabited by ethnic minorities, who also constitute one third of the total population of the western region.

Even when the priority was given to the development of eastern coastal areas in the early years of reform and opening up, the state had not neglected the development of ethnic minority areas. While encouraging certain areas to get rich first, the state also adopted special preferential policies for certain areas including those inhabited by ethnic minorities, and offered necessary material and technical support to them.

In 1995 the state decided that more attention should be attached to the development of the central and western regions, and that policies should be enacted to bridge the widening gap between the east and the west. It also decided that in the next 15 years one of the guiding principles for economic and social development is to accelerate the development of the west, and adopted concrete measures for this purpose. After the western development strategy was formulated, the state adopted more detailed preferential policies for its implementation. Soon several landmark projects were started, such as the west-east gas pipeline, the west-east power transmission project, and the Qinghai-Tibet Railway. These are known as "China's most important projects in the early 21st century." Following them are more projects and deeds, and they are rapidly changing the status quo of ethnic minority areas.

Four. Border trade and opening up of border areas

China's border areas are mostly compact communities of ethnic minorities, with many land ports, and over 30 ethnic minorities live in border areas facing their foreign neighbors of the same ethnic origin. They speak the same languages and share similar folkways,

Engineering machinery being shipped to Xinjiang from other parts of China.

which facilitate external exchange. After the founding of New China in 1949, border trade was stopped for sometime. The trade was resumed after 1978, when China implemented reform and opening up, first from barter trade between people on both sides of the border. Since then the state has formulated preferential policies to promote the development of border trade.

Aidian port in Ningming County of Guangxi used to be a small village with only several hundred people. Thanks to border trade, within only 10 years Aidian built the largest market for trade in traditional Chinese medicine and medicinal herbs on the Sino-Vietnamese border. The Zhuang people there, who used to be farmers for generations, caught the opportunity and became traders. Many people have made good money and built new homes, leading a new life. In Aidian, an industrial park was set up, and goods from the park sell well on both domestic and foreign markets. Similar to

Aidian, most of the 112 border counties in China were haunted by poverty before border trade was launched. Nowadays many counties have increased their revenues and created a lot of job opportunities, and some poverty-stricken counties have turned into enviable "counties of moderate affluence."

In 1992 the state implemented the opening up of border areas and approved the opening of 13 cities in those areas. Governments of these cities have greater powers in managing border trade and economic cooperation, and they can review and approve on their own projects of border trade, processing and labor service cooperation. To attract domestic and foreign investment, some border cities have set up economic cooperation zones, and enterprises in these zones are entitled to preferential policies of the central and local governments and other conveniences.

In the meantime, the national policies of reform and opening up have also been implemented in the ethnic minority areas. In recent years the Chinese government has been implementing a program to rejuvenate the border areas and help people there get rich. This program includes the following tasks: poverty reduction efforts focused on providing enough food and clothing for the indigent people; construction of infrastructure facilities including water supply, electricity, roads and communications; restructuring of industries to cultivate new growth areas and specialized economies; opening to the outside world with regional economic cooperation and border trade as the focus; social progress, including universal nine-year compulsory education, literacy for youngsters and adults, and extension of appropriate technology; development of cultural facilities for invigoration of ethnic minority cultures; and ecological conservation and environmental protection, mainly by retiring fragile fields and switching them to planting trees and grass.

Five. Encouraging economically developed areas to support ethnic minority areas in an one-to-one manner

In 1979 the state decided that economically developed provinces and municipalities should support ethnic minority areas in economic development in a one-to-one manner. It was decided that they should form the following pairs: Beijing-Inner Mongolia, Hebei-Guizhou, Jiangsu-Guangxi/Xinjiang, Shandong-Qinghai, Tianjin-Gansu, and Shanghai-Yunnan/Ningxia; in addition, all other parts of the country should support Tibet. After that, the developed provinces and municipalities provided material and technical assistance to their counterparts and they formed economic alliance. Later the assistance was expanded to cover industry, agriculture, commerce, technology, human resources, culture, education, and health. Meanwhile regional economic cooperation has also expanded, in southwest China an economic cooperation zone of five provinces and seven parties was formed, and in northwest China a five-province/region economic cooperation zone was also formed.

Tibet is a major destination of assistance. In 1984 the state decided that nine provinces and municipalities helped build 43 projects in

A windpower station in Inner Mongolia, a region abounding with wind energy resources.

Tibet with state investment. Since 1994, the central government has made direct investments to build 62 projects in Tibet, and 15 provinces, municipalities and central government departments helped build over 700 projects in Tibet in free economic aid. Over 2,000 officials were sent to Tibet from all parts of the country to help local development.

Six. Assisting ethnic minority areas in poverty reduction

In recent years many ethnic minority areas have made progress in economic development, and people there have got rich. But quite a large number of ethnic minority people are still in poverty. Of these indigent people, about half live in the stony mountain areas in the southwest, and the rest, in northwest China, either in highland areas with a cold climate, in areas suffering desertification, or in dry mountain areas. The poverty there results from various factors: poor natural conditions in some places that are unfit for human beings, remote areas that are far away from major cities and markets, backward infrastructure (including water conservation, energy, transport and communications), and a poor basis of economic, educational and scientific development in history.

To help ethnic minority areas in poverty reduction, the state has adopted special supportive policies.

In designating destinations of assistance, the state sets more flexible standards for ethnic minority areas, and it also gives more funds and materials to poverty-stricken areas inhabited by ethnic minorities than other areas.

The state also adopted preferential financial, taxation and banking policies for ethnic minority areas. For instance, indigent households are exempted from taxes on agricultural or animal husbandry production, preferential treatment is given to people who start businesses, and poverty-stricken counties are allowed to keep their tax revenues after fulfilling taxation tasks.

A silk mill in Hotan, Xinjiang.

Special funds are allotted for development projects aimed at poverty reduction. Such funds include those for solving food and clothing problems in poverty-stricken areas, for comprehensive development of agriculture in such areas, and special subsidies to poverty-stricken counties in pastoral areas for improving their conditions of production and life. In addition, the state also provides support in kind for poverty-stricken areas to build roads, power supply facilities, water conservation projects, and to improve the ecological environment.

In the meantime, the state has also attached great importance to the development of science, technology, and cultural undertakings in poverty-stricken areas to help ethnic minorities develop their human resources.

PROTECTION AND DEVELOPMENT OF CULTURAL HERITAGE

Every minority ethnic group in China has its own long history and unique culture. In Chinese history, cultures of ethnic groups have never been attracting more and more people as they do today. In some remote rural areas, local cultures have been kept intact due to the close environment. However, with impacts of modern civilization, some cultural heritage of ethnic minorities in China has been or is being lost. Under such circumstances, how does China preserve and develop the cultural heritage of its ethnic minorities?

Collection and Collation of Classical Works

In their long years of historical development, minority ethnic groups have accumulated a huge number of classical works, both written and unwritten. Usually ethnic minorities who have a written language would have written classics, and those who have no written language would pass on their classics orally.

In 1982 China began a nationwide campaign to collect, collate and publish classical works of ethnic minorities. During this campaign, the collected classical works were preserved, collated and compiled. Researchers went among local people to collect works that had been privately kept, and those works that had been brought overseas were either purchased back or copied. The researchers also made all efforts to record the unwritten works, which were on the verge of extinction. This campaign was planned and administered by the State Commission of Ethnic Affairs. In 1984 a national office

An elderly editor of *Manas*, the heroic epic of the Kirgiz ethnic group, in an interview with a journalist.

was set up to take charge of the campaign, and later similar offices or agencies were established in 25 provinces, autonomous regions and municipalities, and over 130 prefectures or autonomous prefectures (leagues). Classical works research institutes were also set up in some universities and colleges for ethnic groups or in some ethnic minority areas.

According to statistics available, since 1984 China has collected 120,000 classical works of ethnic minorities, which covered history, literature, folkways, religion and medicine. Among them over 110, 000 have been collated, and over 5,000 have been published. Now each of the 55 ethnic minorities has a written outline of its own history.

Folk Arts

Most of China's ethnic minorities are good singers and dancers. On holidays and major events, they would sing and dance to their hearts' content, and even in daily life they would often sing and dance impromptu. The Tibetans have such a saying, "Those who can talk will sing, and those who can walk will dance." Thus one can imagine that what a huge treasury of folk arts they have. With changes in social life, folk songs and dances of ethnic minorities will naturally change. For instance, as primitive faiths declined, some sacrifice songs and dances have disappeared, and others have changed their nature. The Arere dance of Naxi ethnic group is a good example. This dance was previously performed around the dead to disperse the fear of death and nature, but it has now become something entertaining, with completely different new words for the accompanying songs. For young people, as they now have more chances to meet the opposite sex, love songs and dances are not as important as they used to be.

Despite all this, the ethnic minorities still have well preserved and developed their folk arts, in which the government has played a key role. The 12-piece classical musical work of Muqam of the Uygurs in Xinjiang is a good example. In the late 1940s this work was on the verge of extinction, as only several elderly performers could give a complete show. Later the government set up the Xinjiang Muqam Ensemble and Muqam Research Office, and this ancient work of art was revived and developed. There are still many cases like this.

Indeed, some young people are so indulged in the joy of modern life that they become indifferent to traditional culture. Some of them even hold that wearing colorful homemade garments of their own ethnic groups represents poverty and backwardness. In recent years more and more local governments would organize festivals of ethnic minorities and other annual events of entertainment. As these activities have brought about economic benefits and showed the charm of folk culture, many people have changed their minds, and some young people began to learn the traditional songs and dances

Mongolian folk artists performing the heroic epic *Jangar*.

and handicraft workmanship, introducing some modern elements into them. Folk arts that were once declining are inherited, and new development is made.

Besides the government, some private organizations also play an important role in inheriting and developing traditional culture. The classical Daoist musical work Dongjing has long been lost in northern China, yet it is still quite popular in southwest China's Yunnan Province, where many ethnic minorities live. Dongjing ensembles can be found in various parts of Yunnan, especially in Kunming, Dali and Lijiang. In Dali Bai Autonomous Prefecture, there are more than 340 Dongjing bands, with players from the Bai, Yi and Han ethnic groups, and amateur Dongjing players total more than 10, 000. These amateurs do not perform shows to the public, but they meet in spare time to entertain themselves. Some ensembles are even invited to make performance tours in other parts of China and abroad.

From generation to generation, many fairy tales, folklores and ballads have been circulating among ethnic minorities in China. As early as the 1950s, the government had organized researchers to collect and save these cultural heritages during the investigation of history and language of ethnic minorities. In the early 1980s researchers began the compilation of ten collections of Chinese folk culture, including folk songs, folk tales, proverbs, ballads, folk opera music works, folk Quyi (art forms) music works, folk dances, folk

A Tibetan drama performance.

instrumental music works, annals of Chinese operas, and annals of Chinese folk Quyi art forms. It took 20 years for 50,000 experts and cultural workers to compile 310 volumes of books to record the folk literature and art of China's 56 ethnic groups.

The three major heroic epics of Chinese ethnic minorities – *Gesar* of the Tibetan, *Jangar* of the Mongolian, and *Manas* of the Kirgiz – have been passed down from generation to generation through story-telling and ballad-singing by folk artists. The Tibetan epic of *Gesar* is the largest of its kind in the world, but there are only some 100 folk artists who can tell and sing it, with different oral versions. To preserve these epics, China has established special institutions to collect, collate, translate, publish and study the three epics. To date the three epics have been published in Tibetan, Mongolian, Kirgiz and Chinese languages as well as foreign languages, and also published are some works on their studies. Of the three epics, over 100 versions of *Gesar* have been collected.

Historical Relics and Sites

Ancient Chinese civilization has left numerous relics and historical sites in the country. In many areas inhabited by ethnic minorities, let alone the huge ancient sites, architecture and grottos, even some articles now still being used in daily life or some decorations may be cultural relics themselves in the eyes of archaeologists.

Since the founding of New China, the central and local governments have carried out numerous surveys of cultural relics and historical sites, and put a large number of them under protection. A huge amount of information has been collected, and many publications including annals of cultural relics, survey reports and papers have been produced.

A large number of museums have been built to preserve the cultural relics of ethnic minorities – some are national, others are local; some are for all ethnic groups, and others are for respective ethnic minorities each. The Culture Palace for Nationalities in Beijing is a national museum built in 1959. It stores a great number of cultural relics and often runs exhibitions about ethnic minorities. In 1984 the state decided that a modern, comprehensive museum, the China Museum of Nationalities, be built in Beijing. Preparations for the construction of this museum are now underway.

The Potala Palace – the splendid symbol of Tibetan architecture.

The Tibet Museum was completed and put to use in 1999, with an investment of nearly 100 million yuan by the central government. The buildings of the museum are of the traditional Tibetan style, incorporating elements of Tibetan temples, castles and gardens. But its state-of-the-art equipment is quite modern, including lighting, sound, interpretation, fire protection and monitoring systems. Its audio tourist guide system can provide services in English, Japanese, Han and Tibetan languages. Some non-governmental organizations and individuals have also built a number of museums of ethnic minorities or theme parks of folkways, which combine protection of cultural relics of ethnic minorities with folkway tourism.

The giant-scale protection and maintenance of cultural heritage and historical sites in China today may be unprecedented in Chinese history.

The Potala Palace in Lhasa, capital of Tibet, is the largest and most well preserved palace building in Tibet. The Potala Palace used to be the winter residence for the Dalai Lamas of all generations, and it was listed in 1961among the first groups of historical sites under state protection by the State Council, China's central government.

The palace houses one of the largest treasuries of relics from traditional Tibetan culture. Between 1989 and 1994, the central government spent huge funds on the renovation of the Potala Palace. The decoration of buildings and articles alone consumed 1,000 kg of gold. Mainly Tibetan workers and managers carried out the project, with technical professionals from other parts of China providing guidance for them.

The renovated palace is installed with electronic monitoring and automatic fire protection systems. The enormous information of the palace is now being put into a computer system to facilitate the management and to provide visitors with information retrieval service. In May 1994, experts sent by the World Heritage Committee of the United Nations Educational, Scientific and Cultural Organization inspected the renovated palace, and they held that the design and engineering of the renovation was up to world standards, and the renovation itself is "a wonder in the protection of ancient architecture." By yearend of 1994 the Potala Palace was inscribed on the World Heritage List.

Like the Potala Palace, many historical sites in ethnic minority areas have used computer systems for management, and some even use electronic tickets. The mini CD-ROMs that serve as admission tickets are stored with video images of the sites and even traditional ethnic music.

In urban and rural construction in ethnic minority areas, the government requires that the design of new buildings must keep to the local ethnic styles and characteristics. In downtown Lhasa, there were many old buildings of Tibetan style, but they carried no tap water or toilet room. As they became dilapidated, the government decided to renovate them. During the renovation modern facilities were added to the streets and buildings, but their external appearances remained.

The old town of Lijiang has a history of over 800 years. The town has over 6,000 households, mostly of the Naxi ethnic group. In the early 1950s, the government decided to expand the town. They built a new town near Lijiang and kept the old town intact. Today the old town still keeps its ancient landscape of rivers, bridges and households. In 1997 the town was inscribed on the World Heritage List.

Languages

The Chinese language, or the language of the Han people, is the commonly used language in China. Of the 55 minority ethnic groups, the Hui and Manchu people have been using Chinese, and the 53 others have their own languages. Among them 22 ethnic minorities use 28 languages, with some using more than one language – the Dai people use four languages, and the Mongolian, two. As they have had exchange with the Han people for quite a long time, some ethnic minority people also speak Chinese. In some areas with several ethnic groups, people also speak a local common language. For instance, people of various ethnic groups in Xinjiang usually can speak the Uygur language, most people in Mongolia can speak Mongolian, and in Xishuangbanna of Yunnan people there also speak the Dai language.

In the 1950s China organized large-scale investigations of the languages of ethnic minorities. Based on the investigations, the government helped 10 ethnic minorities to create their own writing

The ancient music of Naxi people in Lijiang of Yunnan Province is known as "living fossil of ancient Chinese music."

systems according to their wishes – the Zhuang, Bouyei, Miao, Yi, Li, Naxi, Lisu, Hani, Va and Dong. The government also helped the Lahu, Jingpo and Dai to design their improved written language systems, and the Uygur and Kazak to reform their writing systems. Some ethnic groups chose to use other ethnic languages that they are familiar with – the Monba and Lhoba decided to use Tibetan. With the development of information technology, computerized word processing and publishing systems have been developed for more than 10 languages, such as Mongolian, Tibetan, Uygur, and Kazak.

The Chinese Constitution stipulates, "The people of all nationalities have the freedom to use and develop their own spoken and written languages." Today, majorities of people of most ethnic minorities use their own languages as the main means of communication. In schools mainly for ethnic minority students, usually bilingual (Chinese and an ethnic minority language) instruction is practiced. In many ethnic autonomous areas, both Chinese and the local ethnic language are used for government documents, meetings, and signs of public places. Ethnic minority languages are also widely used in publishing, broadcasting, television and films. The Central People's Broadcasting Station (China National Radio) has an ethnic minorities department, which broadcasts programs in Mongolian, Tibetan, Uygur, Kazak and Korean to audiences at home and abroad. The television stations of Inner Mongolia, Xinjiang and Tibet have opened channels in local languages. Documents in seven ethnic minority languages – Mongolian, Tibetan, Uygur, Kazak, Korean, Zhuang and Yi – are provided to delegates of relevant ethnic groups at the National Congress of the Communist Party of China, the sessions of the National People's Congress and the National Committee of the Chinese People's Political Consultative Conference. Simultaneous interpretation in these seven languages is also provided at such meetings.

The Constitution provides that in performing their functions, the organs of self-government of the ethnic autonomous areas, in accordance with the autonomy regulations of the respective areas, employ the spoken and written language or languages in common use in the locality. Some ethnic autonomous areas have enacted rules on the use of ethnic languages. Tibetan Autonomous Region stipulates that the Tibetan language is the main language, and both Tibetan and Chinese are used.

The Chinese Constitution also provides that citizens of all ethnic groups have the right to use the spoken and written languages of their own ethnic groups in court proceedings. The people's courts and people's procuratorates should provide translation for any party to the court proceedings who is not familiar with the spoken or written languages in common use in the locality. In an area where people of a minority ethnic group live in a compact community or where a number of ethnic groups live together, hearings should be conducted in the language or languages in common use in the locality; indictments, judgments, notices and other documents should be written, according to actual needs, in the language or languages in common use in the locality.

Horse racing, a festival activity for Kazaks in Xinjiang.

Traditional Medicine and Sports

All ethnic groups in China have their own traditional medicine. In many areas, such as Miao communities in Guizhou, many people can recognize several or even tens of medicinal herbs and know how to use them, and it has become a folkway for people to recognize, collect, use and grow medicinal herbs. As one of their folk songs sings, "The Miao medicine has a history of one thousand or even ten thousand years." This proves the long history of traditional medicine. Some ethnic minorities have not only rich experience in medical practice but also systematic medical knowledge, and their medical classics have been inherited by current practitioners. Others have passed down their medical knowledge orally from generation to generation, and such knowledge has yet to be tapped, summed up and developed.

Such a situation has changed greatly in the past half a century and more and especially in the past two decades and more. The research and development of traditional medicine of ethnic minorities has become a passion in Chinese medical circles. With investments from the central government or local governments, over 100 hospitals featuring medicine of ethnic minorities have been set up in various parts of the country, with a majority of them being of Tibetan, Mongolian or Uygur medicine. And many other areas have set up specialized hospitals or clinics featuring medicine of ethnic minorities, or specialized departments featuring such medicine in ordinary hospitals.

Ethnic minority areas have set up research institutions to collect and collate local medicine classics, carry out experiments and develop medicine products. To date a number of classical works and proved recipes have been compiled and published. Researchers have also developed several hundred products based on traditional medicine and using modern pharmaceutical technology. These products are sold on the home market and exported to other countries. A number of domestic and foreign investors have taken part in the development of traditional medicine of ethnic minorities.

The state has also set up colleges of local traditional medicine in Tibet, Inner Mongolia and Xinjiang. Excellent experts of traditional medicine are organized to cultivate successors. A large number of workers in local traditional medicine have been brought up through education in vocational schools and colleges, on-the-job training, study tours to other parts of the country and to other countries, and private tutoring.

Traditional sports of ethnic minorities in China have a long history, and they are in numerous forms. They have three salient features. First, the sports are closely related to production activities. The Mongolian, Tibetan and Kazak people are traditionally herdsmen on grasslands, and they had to ride horses and be good archers, hence the sports of horsemanship and horse racing. Ethnic minorities who engaged in agriculture or both farming and hunting or collecting would have mountaineering, wrestling, archery and other hand skills as their traditional sports. Second, they are closely related to folk customs. Many of the sports are thus passed down and developed, especially those practiced on festivals and celebrations. For instance, for the traditional Mongolian festival of Nadam, wrestling, horse racing and archery are the three indispensable sports. Likewise, dragon boating is necessary for the Dai people at the Water-Splashing Festival, and wrestling is a must for the Yi people at their Torchlight Festival. Third, many sports are integrated with song and dance. The sports of Jumping over Bamboo Rods of the Li people and the Jumping under the Moon of the Yi people are all accompanied by song and dance. Fourth, all the sports are easy to carried out without special grounds and equipment, and

Satellite antenna dishes enable ethnic minority people in mountain areas to know about the outside world through radio and television broadcasts.

they do not take a lot of financial and material resources.

In the past, sports of ethnic minorities were left for them to grow or die on their own. In 1953 China launched its first national games of ethnic minority sports. In 1982 the second national games of such sports were held, and the central government decided that the event would be open every four years in future. Since then, the five autonomous regions and most provinces and municipalities, as well as other ethnic minority areas, have held similar sports events on a regular or non-regular basis. With years of efforts, some sports items that were once extinct have been revived, some have been listed among national games, and others have been reformed. In some ethnic minority areas, local schools also list local traditional sports among their physical education.

CHINA

Developing Modern Cultural Facilities

In the early years of the People's Republic, many ethnic minority areas were rather backward culturally, without any library, culture center, or radio and television service. Now things have changed greatly. Virtually every village in China is covered by radio and television broadcast service, and many ethnic minority areas have their own programs and channels in local languages. In pastoral areas on grasslands, mobile culture stations are set up for herdsmen, and they show movies and video programs, rent books, sell goods, repair home appliances, and even perform shows. Since the 1990s, the state has been implementing a program to improve cultural facilities in border areas. With funds from the central and local governments, ethnic minorities built, expanded and renovated a large number of libraries, culture centers, museums and theaters. There are now several hundred newspapers and magazines either in ethnic minority languages or catering to ethnic minorities, including national ones and those run by ethnic autonomous areas. Of the over 500 publishing houses in the country, 36 are related to ethnic minorities. The state subsidizes publications in ethnic minority languages, and prizes are regularly awarded to Best Books for Ethnic Minorities in China.

Since the 1950s a number of ethnic minority art troupes, both professional and amateur, have been set up. In Beijing, the national Central Song and Dance Troupe of Ethnic Groups is composed of actors and actresses from all ethnic groups, and it mainly performs songs and dances of ethnic minorities to audiences throughout the country. In 1957 the first Ulanmuqi – a cultural troupe mounted on horseback – was founded in Inner Mongolia, where herdsmen lived scattered in pastoral areas. Later more and more such troupes were set up, members of these troupes give performances and also teach amateurs, collect folk art heritage, and sell books. They are in fact cultural work teams. Since the reform and opening up began in 1978, herdsmen in Inner Mongolia have greatly improved their cultural life, yet the Ulanmuqi troupes are still widely welcomed. Wherever they go, local herdsmen would treat them like distinguished guests. Currently there are over 500 art performance troupes in ethnic autonomous areas in China.

Since the founding of New China in 1949, the state has trained numerous personnel in ethnic minority culture. At present 24 national colleges and universities run classes for culture and art of ethnic minorities. Such specialties as literature, music, dance and fine arts of ethnic minorities are also available in schools for ethnic minority students and institutions of higher learning in ethnic autonomous areas.

MODERN EDUCATION

Before the 1950s education of ethnic minorities in China was rather backward. Some ethnic minorities who were still in a primitive stage of social development had no schools or teachers, and they simply passed on their production skills and folkways personally from generation to generation. Certain ethnic minorities carried on their religion-oriented education in temples. Although over 30 ethnic minorities began modern schooling in the early 20th century, there were few schools and students. Half a century ago illiteracy was as high as over 90% among adults of ethnic minorities, especially among women.

In 2001 this author met an elderly man in Jiejinkou Township, the compact community of the Hezhens in Tongjiang City of Heilongjiang Province. Although the old man could not even write his own name, he was very proud of his offspring, "I'm too old and cannot read or write. But my children and grand children are promising – my youngest grand child is at primary school, and the two eldest are at college."

In 1949, the year the People's Republic was founded, the Hezhen population was merely 300, with over 90% of them illiterate. In 1950 Jiejinkou Township set up the first primary school for Hezhens. From among its graduates grew the first officials, teachers and scholars of Hezhen ethnicity in China.

Today the Hezhen population is over 4,500, and illiterates among those under 45 years have dropped to less than 2%. The first primary school has been expanded to offer pre-school education and junior

A class in an ethnic school in Xinjiang.

middle school classes apart from primary education. Its campus covers some 10,000 square meters, with two rows of brick buildings. The school has now chemistry and physics labs, a library, and a clinic, and it has also computers.

In China, all ethnic groups are equal in education. The development of education is related to economic, cultural and social development in a locality. As education is relatively backward in ethnic minority areas, the government has adopted preferential policies to support education in those areas.

Administration of Education

In the early 1950s organs in charge of education in ethnic minority areas were established in the Ministry of Education under the Central People's Government and in educational administration departments of governments at various levels. At present the Ministry of Education has the department of ethnic minorities education, and the State Commission of Ethnic Affairs has the department of education. These two departments are jointly responsible for the administration and guidance of education in ethnic minority areas. The education departments of some provinces and regions with a large population of ethnic minorities have also set up relevant organs.

Mongolian pupils playing on a campus.

Under the guidance of unified principles and policies for education, the central government gives the ethnic autonomous areas the power to independently develop education. The Constitution provides that the organs of self-government of ethnic autonomous areas shall independently develop education for the localities, decide on the plans for the development of education in these areas, on the establishment of various kinds of schools at different levels, on their educational system, forms, curricula, the language used in instruction and enrollment procedures.

Forms of Schooling

Chinese schools of various kinds and at all levels are open to students of all ethnic groups. Besides ordinary schools, many areas also run ethnic schools or classes for ethnic minority students.

Ethnic schools enroll mainly students of ethnic minorities but they also have a small number of Han students. They include primary and high schools and also vocational schools. An ethnic school may be set up for a single ethnic group or for a number of ethnic groups. Such schools are set up not to limit students of ethnic minorities to them, but that they may get special support in assigning teaching staff, in teaching conditions and in using ethnic languages for instruction. Students may voluntarily choose to attend ordinary schools or ethnic schools.

In remote areas with sparse population and poor transport facilities including pastoral areas, local governments have set up boarding schools for primary and secondary education. Students live in such schools on government stipends, and they are exempted from tuitions and other fees or pay only a small sum. Such boarding schools are funded by provincial, prefecture or county governments. The central government also extends support to them in funding, teaching staff and equipment.

As a supplement to regular schools, electronic education is developing rapidly in ethnic minority areas. Over 70% of the counties in China have set up their own television stations (relay stations) for education. Most of the ethnic schools can use audio-and-video materials and radio and television networks in teaching and in training of teachers. In some areas with good conditions, intra-school computer networks have been set up, which are linked to the national distance education network so that they can share information resources.

There are 13 ethnic institutions of higher learning in China. These institutions are different from regular ones in that apart from education for college students they also offer training for officials and have preparatory departments. When they were set up in the 1950s, they mainly engaged in training of ethnic officials rather than cultivating professionals. Since 1979 they have attached equal attention to both tasks. Apart from ethnically oriented disciplines, these institutions also offer regular courses, such as humanities, science, industry, agriculture, medicine, arts, and management. The charges of ethnic schools are lower than other colleges in the locality, and students of ethnic disciplines are exempted from tuition fees and entitled to higher stipends.

In quite a number of institutions of higher learning and vocational secondary schools, there are preparatory classes for students of ethnic minorities. These students would study for one year if they are of relatively high educational attainment, and for two years if they still have to learn the Chinese language. Students from these classes who are qualified in examinations will enter or continue their studies at college.

In addition, in some universities, colleges and vocational schools there are also special classes of ethnic minority students. In some areas where there is a low enrollment of girl students due to traditional bias against girls, special classes or schools for girls are set up to change the situation.

Ethnic Language Instruction and Bilingual Instruction

The Law on Ethnic Regional Autonomy of China provides that Schools where most of the students come from minority ethnic groups should, whenever possible, use textbooks in their own languages and use these languages as the media of instruction.

Classes for the teaching of Chinese (the Han language) shall be opened for senior grades of primary schools or for secondary schools to popularize *Putonghua*, the common speech based on Beijing pronunciation, and the standardized Chinese characters.

Due to the different situations in the use of both spoken and written languages of ethnic groups in various areas, the use of ethnic languages for instruction and bilingual instruction falls into three categories. One. For ethnic minorities who have their own spoken language but not written language or for ethnic minorities having their own written language but in the areas where they live Chinese is the common written language, the schools use both Chinese and ethnic languages for instruction, but no classes in ethnic written languages are given. Two. For ethnic minorities who have their own written languages that are widely used, the schools use two languages for instruction, and both Chinese and ethnic written languages are

Daur students learning to use the computer.

taught, with focus on the ethnic minority languages. Three. For ethnic minorities who have both spoken and written languages of their own but use Chinese more often, the schools use both Chinese and ethnic languages for instruction, and both Chinese and ethnic written languages are taught, with focus on Chinese. As things are different in various localities, schools would decide on their own when to teach the courses of Chinese and ethnic languages and how long the courses will last. Bilingual instruction is also practiced in some vocational schools, colleges and ethnic colleges in ethnic autonomous areas.

Currently over 10,000 schools for 21 ethnic minorities in 13 provinces and autonomous regions use ethnic minority languages or both Chinese and ethnic minority languages for instruction, and these schools have over 6 million students. The ethnic minority languages used number more than 60.

The state has set up publishing institutions in relevant provinces and autonomous regions to compile and translate textbooks in ethnic languages, and organized three inter-provincial networks for publishing textbooks. Governments at all levels provide financial support for publications in ethnic languages.

Financial Support for Education

As many ethnic schools are situated in remote, mountainous or pastoral areas and they have to use both Chinese and ethnic minority languages for instruction, they need more funds to cover their expenses than ordinary schools. In addition, ethnic minority areas are usually economically backward and their financial resources are insufficient for the development of education, therefore they need financial support from the state. Even in the early years of the People's Republic, when the state finance faced difficulties, ethnic minority

Minority students in Yunnan learning to speak *Putonghua*, the common speech in China.

areas had got special funding for ethnic education in addition to regular funds for education. In 1983 the education system was reformed and localities began to be responsible for funding elementary education. Taking into consideration of the conditions in ethnic minority areas, the state began in 1985 allocating 100 million yuan a year for remote, mountainous, border and indigent areas to develop primary education. Of the total, over 50% goes to eight provinces and autonomous regions with a large ethnic minority population, including Xinjiang and Inner Mongolia. In 1990 the Ministry of Finance decided that beginning in that year an annual allocation of 20 million yuan would go to subsidize education in ethnic minority areas. In 1995 the state set up a special fund for developing compulsory education in indigent areas inhabited by ethnic minorities. In 1997 the state established compulsory education stipends to help children from indigent families finish their schooling, especially children of ethnic minorities. At the same time, some provinces and autonomous regions have also established special funds for subsidizing ethnic education. Apart from all this, the state also makes use of World Bank assistance and donations for the Hope Project from all sectors of society to improve elementary education in ethnic minority areas.

CHINA

One-to-One Support for Education

As the ethnic minority areas have poor infrastructure for education, they need assistance from the state and support from other provinces as well. The one-to-one support for education in ethnic minority areas began in the 1950s, and it has increased greatly since the 1980s.

The one-to-one support for education includes many aspects. One is to provide funds, materials, teaching instruments and equipment, and books to indigent areas for them to improve elementary education, vocational education, literacy education and technical training for adults, and to help dropouts to continue their schooling. Another is to send teachers and education administrators to teach and work in indigent areas, to help indigent counties work out their overall plans for education including various specialized education programs, to pass experience and information on educational reform and administration of education, and to help indigent areas better allocate their education resources. Still another is to train teachers, administrators, technical professionals and managers for indigent areas. Finally one-to-one support also will launch cooperative

Bai pupils learning to play the violin.

enterprises run by schools that take less investment, yield good benefits and are competitive, plus exchange of information and transfer of technology, to help education institutions in indigent areas enhance their capability of self-improvement.

As Tibet is somewhat in seclusion in terms of education and lacks various professionals, the state pays special attention to the development of education there. In 1984, the central government decided that apart from improving education in Tibet Autonomous Region, special high schools and classes for Tibetan students would be launched in other parts of the country to enroll 1,300 to 1,500 Tibetan students a year, mainly for training secondary technical professionals. For this program, the central government allocated 185 million yuan for construction and equipment, and relevant local governments also spent over 200 million yuan on the construction of the schools. In addition, the local governments provide an annual allowance of 3,500 to 9,000 yuan for each Tibetan student from the local budget, to subsidize the students' expenses on study and daily life. The special high schools and classes for Tibetan students practice bilingual instruction, and Tibet Autonomous Region sends Tibetan teachers and administrators to work in them. Most graduates from these schools and classes enter vocational schools, and some are enrolled in institutions of higher learning. Currently there are over 150 such schools (classes) in 26 provinces, autonomous regions and municipalities, with some 15,000 Tibetan students. Beginning in 2000, the central government decided to launch senior high school classes for students from Xinjiang in 12 cities in the eastern region, including Beijing and Shanghai. The first year these classes enrolled 1,000 graduates of various ethnic groups from junior high schools in Xinjiang.

Preferential Treatment for Students of Ethnic Minorities

In enrolling students, institutions of higher learning and vocational secondary schools give preferential treatment to applicants of ethnic minorities. Various provinces, autonomous regions and municipalities have different standards for the preferential treatment, but usually the qualified marks for applicants of ethnic minorities are lower. Some localities set ratios and different qualified marks for applicants of ethnic minorities and Han applicants respectively. The difference in qualified marks may be smaller for ethnic minorities that have good education background and larger for those with poorer educational attainment. And ethnic minorities with smaller populations get more special treatment.

As many students of ethnic minorities come from remote areas with backward economies, their families usually have difficulties in supporting them. Therefore the state gives special assistance to students of ethnic minorities. The law provides that students in compulsory education are charged no tuition fees except for other expenses, but students of ethnic minorities are not charged for any fees. In institutions of higher learning, students are charged for tuition fees and other expenses, but students in ethnic minority-oriented specialties who get scholarship from the state are charged for no tuition fees.

For a long period since the 1950s, government stipends were given to students in institutions of higher learning and high schools, and students of ethnic minorities got a bit more than their Han counterparts. Later this stipend system was reformed. Beginning in 1987 scholarships and student loans were enforced in colleges and universities, with scholarships for excellent students, certain specialties and certain destinations of graduates. But all students enrolled in ethnic schools (specialties) are entitled to scholarships. In many boarding and semi-boarding primary and high schools, students still get monthly stipends.

CUSTOMS AND RELIGIONS

Ethnic groups in China have various habits and customs regarding production, food, residence, garments, marriage, funerals, festivals, entertainment, protocols, and taboos, which are highly ethnicity-specific. These habits and customs have gradually changed in history. As people shift from traditional farming, pasturing, fishing and hunting to modern way of life, the changes in habits and customs become more remarkable.

Take the Mongolian people for example. The Mongolians used to live a nomad life on grasslands. They wore Mongolian gowns and boots, rode horses, ate beef, mutton and milk products, and lived in yurts, which can be easily installed and dismantled. Now more and more Mongolians have entered towns and cities, engaged in new professions, and wear modern garments. Those who still herd animals for a living no longer move from place to place searching for water and grass, but live in warm houses, use coal and gas for cooking, and own home appliances. The Mongolians used to be known as "an ethnic group on horseback," but nowadays horses are disappearing, in their place are motorcycles and cars. This situation is what people who love horses are unwilling to see but have to face. As more and more vehicles and machines are used in agriculture and animal husbandry on grasslands, the market for horses is shrinking, and fewer herdsmen are now raising horses.

Despite all this, Mongolians still keep their folkways. During holidays they would wear ethnic garments and entertain themselves with songs and dances. Whenever guests come, Mongolians would

Water-splashing Festival of the Dai people.

gallantly present them with wine and sing welcome songs. On grasslands in northern China, wherever Mongolians live there will be Nadam fairs, which feature sacrifice, contests, entertainment and well-wishing, usually held in summer and autumn. Previously Nadam fairs were organized by tribes or governments. Now Mongolian herdsmen who have got rich themselves also hold small-scale Nadam fairs – to celebrate their children being enrolled in college, hail good harvests of animals, or wish elderly relatives good health on birthdays for longevity.

The state laws provide that all ethnic groups have the freedom to keep or reform their habits and customs. Relevant policies have been enacted to enforce the provisions.

Respect for the Food-and-Drink Customs of Ethnic Minorities

Ethnic minorities in China have different food-and-drink customs. The state has taken measures to ensure the production and supply of special foods for ethnic minorities, especially the 10 Moslem ethnic groups of Hui, Uygur, Kazak, Kirgiz, Tajik, Tatar, Uzbek, Dongxiang, Salar and Bonan.

At government departments, schools, enterprises and institutions where there are a large number of people who are on Moslem food, a special Moslem canteen or counter will be set up. Those units with

A Moslem restaurant in Shanghai.

a small number of Moslem people will share a canteen with nearby units or have specialized cooking utensils for them. In cities, catering and retailing outlets for Moslem food are widely distributed. Apart from Moslem restaurants, Moslem food is also supplied in hotels and hospitals, and on trains and airplanes. When one declares to be on Moslem food, such food will be supplied. The state requires that Moslem foods must be marked "Qingzhen" (Chinese for Moslem), so that they can be stored, shipped and sold separately. In large and medium cities with compact communities of Moslem ethnic groups, wholesale and retail shops for beef and mutton are set up. The state also gives preferential treatment to Moslem food production and marketing enterprises. For quite a long period before the 1990s there was a shortage of supplies of commodities in China, and many goods were rationed. At that time the government gave preferential treatment to ethnic minority people in the supply of beef, mutton, rice and zanba, a Tibetan food made of qingke barley flour. Now as supplies are ample, those policy measures are no longer needed, but their guiding spirit is still alive.

Respect for the Clothing Customs of Ethnic Minorities

Ethnic minorities in China have their own traditional garments and costumes. Nowadays people of ethnic minorities mostly wear modern garments in their daily life. But that does not mean that traditional garments have disappeared. The situation is different with different ethnic groups, different areas, and people of different age groups. Usually on ethnic festivals, weddings, funerals and tourist activities, ethnic minority people would put on their traditional costumes.

Garments and costumes of ethnic minorities have their own special features. For instance, Tibetan, Mongolian and Kazak people usually wear gowns and boots; women of Miao, Yi, Tibetan and other ethnic groups love to wear gold and silver ornaments; and people of Bonan, Tibetan, Mongolian and other minorities often carry knives on their waist. The government has made special regulations and arrangements to meet their needs. In many areas of the country, special stores or counters for ethnic goods are set up. For a long period of time, the Chinese government exercised strict control on the purchase and marketing of gold and silver, but it also allocated quotas of gold and silver for the production of ornaments for ethnic minorities, and allowed private craftsmen in ethnic minority areas

Miao girls going to the Sisters' Festival in a mountain area in Guizhou.

to process gold and silver articles for local people. The government exercises control on certain kinds of knives such as daggers, but their production and sales are allowed in ethnic minority areas. To ensure the supply of special goods for ethnic minorities, the state has formulated a catalogue of them and designated producers and marketers, and it also offers preferential loans and pricc subsidies on these goods.

Respect for the Observation of Festivals of Ethnic Minorities

Due to their different history, culture and religion traditions, ethnic groups in China have a large number of festivals of their own, such as the Tibetan New Year, the Water-Splashing Festival of the Dai, the Torchlight Festival of the Yi, and the Lesser Bairam and Qurban festivals for Moslem ethnic groups. Historically there were numerous ethnic festivals; for instance Naxi people had a festival every month. At present, major ethnic festivals are still observed, but many festivals related to primitive religions have either disappeared or declined.

Other festivals have added new features. In recent years, as local governments began to sponsor traditional festival activities, some of the ethnic festivals have grown in scale.

As stipulated by the state, local governments of ethnic minority areas decide the legal holidays of traditional festivals in accordance with the ethnic customs. For instance, the Qurban is a major traditional festival for Moslem ethnic groups. As the Qurban comes around the New Year, the Uygur, Tajik and other minorities in Xinjiang observe this festival as a New Year celebration, making this religious event more joyous. On the day Moslem believers bathe and wear new garments, attend ceremonies at mosques, and remember their ancestors. The Moslems there have a three-day holiday, and they visit relatives and friends, and hold various celebrations.

Respect for the Funeral Customs of Ethnic Minorities

Ethnic groups in China have various funeral customs. Moslem ethnic groups like the Hui practice inhumation, the Tibetans, celestial

Escorting the bride – a folk custom of Miao people on Hainan Island.

burial, and other groups, water burial or cremation. The state respects the funeral customs of ethnic minorities, while encouraging the Han people to practice cremation. In some areas cemeteries for the Hui people are built, and special funeral services are offered. In Tibet, the government protects the grounds for celestial burial as required by Tibetan residents.

Prohibiting Violations of Ethnic Customs

Some mass media sometimes mistakenly violate customs of ethnic minorities in their reporting or programs. To solve the problem, the government has time and again issued orders and circulars, urging mass media workers to study the state's ethnic affairs policies, and to understand and respect the customs of ethnic minorities. The government requires that mass media workers should go to ethnic minority areas to make investigations, and that they should be responsible in their reporting, never distort ethnic customs or insult them.

In daily life, some people may say or do something unintentionally violating customs of ethnic minorities due to lack of relevant knowledge. Such people will be criticized and educated to correct the mistakes. But those who intentionally violate customs of ethnic minorities with their violations leading to serious consequences will be prosecuted for their criminal responsibility. The Supreme People's Procuratorate stipulates that the following will be subject to prosecution: those who force ethnic minorities to change their customs or illegally intervene in or sabotage customs of ethnic minorities, resulting in ethnic conflicts, and those who illegally deprive citizens' right to religious beliefs or who encroach on ethnic minorities' customs or habits, leading to other serious consequences. The Criminal Law of the People's Republic of China provides,

The annual Festival for the Elderly of the Korean ethnic group.

"Workers of state organs who illegally deprive citizens' right to religious beliefs or who encroach on minority nationalities' customs or habits, if the case is serious, are to be sentenced to two years or fewer in prison or put under criminal detention."

Respect for the Freedom of Ethnic Minorities to Keep or Reform Their Customs

The ethnic minorities have carried on many fine traditional customs, which are compatible with modern society. For example, many ethnic minorities have a tradition of respecting the aged and loving the young, giving warm reception to guests, and respecting nature. But some customs are incompatible or even harmful.

The government adopts a policy of differentiation towards the customs of ethnic minorities: some are respected, some are left alone, and others are either to be reformed or removed voluntarily by local people with encouragement from the government. For instance, the Torchlight Festival of the Yi people and the Nadam fair of the Mongolians feature respectively singing, dancing, horse racing, bullfighting, wrestling, archery, tug-of-war, and swinging. These items are all inherited and even developed. Horse race, wrestling and archery have been listed among sports games and got support from the government.

In the south, some ethnic minorities such as the Dai, Zhuang and Bouyei used to live upstairs in two-story piled buildings, with their cattle and pigs kept downstairs. This housing arrangement is not so pleasant to the eye, and detrimental to people's health. With assistance from the government, local people renovated the houses by building separate sheds for animals. In this way the old houses are kept and become cleaner.

In Yongning area of Ninglang Yi Autonomous County in Yunnan Province, people used to keep a primitive marriage system called Zouhun (visiting marriage), which is a remnant of primitive maternal society. After the founding of New China, the government encouraged monogamy, but did not force local people to change their way of marriage; instead it guided local people to reform the system by publicity efforts. Nowadays some people there have voluntarily adopted monogamy, and others still follow the visiting marriage. In some areas inhabited by the Yi and Jingpo people, there used to be a practice of seizing a woman for a man to marry. This practice was long given up after the founding of New China as local people found it to be detrimental to intra-ethnic group unity. Other unhealthy customs have also been reformed by various ethnic minorities, such as early marriage and early birth, mercenary marriage, polygamy, men keeping away from planting rice seedlings and women from plowing, and slaughtering cattle for sacrifice to ghosts. But all the reforms were made gradually and voluntarily.

Airing the Buddha Painting, a traditional festival for Tibetan Buddhism.

Respect for and Protection of the Freedom of Religious Belief of the Ethnic Minorities

China is a country where a number of religions coexist. Major faiths include Buddhism, Daoism, Islam, Catholicism and Christianity, and there are also Shamanism, Orthodox Church, and the Dongba religion. Religious believers total over 100 million in China. Most of the ethnic minorities have religions and some groups are all believers. Different ethnic groups and different people may believe in different religions. The 10 ethnic minorities of Hui, Uygur, Kazak, Kirgiz, Tatar, Uzbek, Tajik, Dongxiang, Salar and Bonan believe in Islam; the Tibetan, Mongolian, Lhoba, Monba, Tu, Yugur people believe in Tibetan Buddhism (Lamaism); the Dai, Blang and De'ang people believe in Hinayana Buddhism; and some people of the Miao, Yao and Yi ethnic groups are Catholic or Christian. Among all religions, Tibetan Buddhism and Islam have the largest numbers

A Moslem prayer in a mosque.

of ethnic minorities and believers.

China enforces a policy for freedom of religious belief. To believe in or not to believe in any religion is up to the personal choice of citizens, and no state organ, public organization or individual should compel any people in this respect. Religious believers and nonbelievers are equal before the law, and they enjoy equal rights and shoulder equal duties under the law. The state protects normal religious activities. All normal activities at religious sites and in the homes of believers are conducted by religious organizations and believers themselves, and such activities are protected by law and free from intervention by any individual. In China, no religion is in a special position, and the government treats all religions equally without discrimination. Believers of all religions are encouraged to respect each other and live in harmony. Religion is separated from state power and from education. The organs of state power do not use religion to serve themselves, and religion does not interfere in administration, justice and education. All religions are independent and self-run.

There have been quite a few untrue reports on religions in China in the foreign press. As a matter of fact, the Chinese government pays special attention to respecting and protecting the freedom of religious belief for all ethnic groups. Take Tibet for example. Most Tibetans believe in Tibetan Buddhism. The region now has over 1, 700 Buddhist religious sites, with over 46,000 monks and nuns in lamaseries. The households of believers have small scripture halls or Buddhist niches. Every year over one million believers would come to Lhasa on pilgrimage. Since the 1980s the central government allocated over 200 million yuan for Tibet to renovate Buddhist temples and special funding for the publication of Tibetan Tripitaka and other Buddhist classics. The government also set up the China Advanced Institute of Tibetan Buddhism in Beijing and the Tibet Buddhist Institute in Lhasa.

In Xinjiang, there are now over 23,000 mosques and 29,000 Islamic religious workers. The region has an Islamic institute for the training of advanced Islamic professionals. The prefectures and cities have also set up Islamic classes for the training of Islamic religious workers. To provide reading materials for religious believers, relevant government departments have organized experts to translate and publish the Koran and other Islamic publications, as well as Buddhist and Christian classics in the Uygur, Kazak, Chinese and other languages. Special outlets for the circulation of religious publications have been set up for the convenience of believers. Since the 1980s over 40,000 Chinese Moslems have made pilgrimage to Mecca, and relevant government departments have provided services for these pilgrims.

Just like the case in Tibet and Xinjiang, the state also respects and protects religious beliefs of other ethnic minorities in other areas.

Mongolian

The Mongolians or Mongols, population: 5,813,900 (2000 census). The Mongolians mainly live in northern China.

In the early 13th century, Genghis Khan unified the tribes in the Mongolian area and established the unitary Mongol empire. In 1279 the Mongol empire unified China and established the Yuan dynasty, which had a territory larger than any previous Chinese dynasties. In 1368 the Yuan dynasty met its destruction. Inner Mongolian Autonomous Region was established in 1947, as the largest Mongolian community in China.

The Mongolians have long been known as "an ethnic group on horseback," and their traditional mode of production was pasturing and hunting. Mongolian herdsmen used to move from place to place searching for water and grass, and they lived in yurts that can be easily installed and dismantled. Now most Mongolians have settled down in brick or earthen houses, and they use motorcycles and automobiles to replace horses for transport.

A Mongolian woman.

Mongolians are good singers and dancers. They have their own language, and most believe in Lamaism. The Mongolian epic *Jangar* is one of the three major heroic epics in China. The traditional Mongolian medicine is best known for its surgery, healing open wounds and broken bones. Mongolians used to wear gowns and boots, which have now become costumes on festivals and tourist activities. The Mongolian diet features beef, mutton, milk products, parched rice, and tea with milk. Mongolians celebrate the Spring Festival and other traditional holidays, and they also hold Nadam fairs in July and August. Nadam means "entertainment" and "games" in Mongolian. Such fairs include wrestling, horse racing, archery, song and dance, and trade in commodities.

Manchu

The Manchus, population: 10,682,300 (2000 census), the second largest among China's 55 ethnic minorities. The Manchu people mainly live in the Northeast, with the largest community in Liaoning Province, and the rest are scattered in various parts of the country.

The Manchus set up the Qing dynasty – the last feudal empire in China – in 1644. The dynasty was exterminated in 1911.

Historically Manchu people engaged mainly in agriculture, fishing and hunting, and they were good at horsemanship and archery. Nowadays riding and archery have declined, but the songs, dances and sports like weightlifting have passed down from generation to generation. The Manchu people are greatly influenced by the

Manchu girls.

culture of the Han people. There have been quite a few Manchu writers, painters and artists, such as Cao Xueqin, the author of the classical novel *The Dream of the Red Chamber*, and modern writer Lao she. Although the Manchus have their own language, as they have lived among the Han people, they now use Chinese. Only a few of them can speak Manchu.

Over a century ago, male Chinese wore long pigtails, which was a custom forced on them by the Qing rulers. Later Manchu men took to the garmenting custom of the Han. Cheongsam, a close-fitting dress with high neck and slit skirt for Manchu women, has become a traditional garment for Chinese women after repeated improvements.

The Manchus used to believe in Shamanism. They believed everything has a soul, and they hated killing dogs or eating dog's meat. Later Buddhism has had considerable influence on them, but the most influential among them is still ancestor worship. The Manchus share many festivals with the Han, such as the Spring Festival, Lantern Festival, Dragon Boat Festival, and Mid-autumn Festival.

Korean

The Koreans, population: 1,923,800 (2000 census). The Koreans in China mainly live in the three northeastern provinces of Jilin, Liaoning and Heilongjiang, and a small number of them reside in Inner Mongolia and some large and medium cities in other parts of the country. Yanbian Korean Autonomous Prefecture of Jilin Province is the major compact community of Koreans in China.

Some Koreans began to move to China from the Korean Peninsula in the 17th century. Their traditional mode of production was agriculture, especially rice farming.

Most Koreans use the Korean language, both spoken and written, and they attach great importance to education. Korean teachers are highly respected. In 1949 Yanbian Ethnic Minority University was set up, the first of its kind in China. Koreans have an educational attainment higher than the average of other ethnic groups in the country.

A Korean girl.

Koreans are highly courteous. Their tradition stresses kindness on the part of parents and filial piety on the part of children, as well as respect for the aged and love for the young. In various Korean communities, there is almost always a festival for the elderly, but at different times of the year. The festival for the elderly in Yanbian is August 15 as designated by the prefecture authorities. Many localities have established associations of the elderly, and they often sponsor various sports and recreation activities. Koreans love songs and dances. Traditional sports include seesaw jumping and swings for women, and wrestling and football for men. Koreans used to wear white clothes, addressing each other as "kinsman (woman) in white". The typical garment for women is a short blouse and a long skirt. Their traditional staple food is rice, and Korean cold noodles, pickled vegetables and barbecue are quite well known.

Korean festivals are much the same as those of the Han. Besides, Koreans also celebrate three family events: the first birthday anniversary of a baby, the sixtieth birthday of an elderly, and the sixtieth wedding anniversary of a couple.

Hezhen

The Hezhens, population: 4,600 (2000 census). The Hezhens mainly live along the Heilong, Wusuli and Songhua rivers in the Northeast.

For generations the Hezhens lived on fishing and hunting, but today professional Hezhen fishermen are few. By the late 1940s the Hezhen population was merely about 300, and the ethnic group was on the verge of extinction.

Hezhens used to make clothes out of fish skin and hides, and they were known as "the fish-skin tribe." In modern times cotton cloth has taken their place, and fish-skin garments have become a specialty handicraft article for tourists.

A Hezhen girl.

The Hezhens have their own spoken language but not a written one, and most Hezhens use Chinese instead. There are many Hezhen folklores, mostly about the origin of Hezhen people, their heroes, places and things, and religious belief. The most noted among them is the Yimakan narrative poems, which have been compiled in over 50 volumes and known as "a living fossil of oral art in northern Asia." Most Yimakan poems are told and some are sung, and it takes several days to complete some long ones.

The Spring Festival is a traditional holiday for the Hezhens. In 1985 the Hezhens launched a new festival, Wurigong, featuring recreation and sports activities. This new festival is held every two years, usually in June or July, lasting three days. During the Wurigong, there are sports games, Yimakan ballads, and feasts for the masses.

Daur

A Daur girl.

The Daurs, population: 132,400 (2000 census). The Daurs mainly reside in compact communities in Inner Mongolia Autonomous Region and Heilongjiang Province, and a small number live in Tacheng County in Xinjiang.

Of all ethnic minorities in northern China, the Daurs were among the first to shift to agriculture from nomadic life or fishing and hunting. However, they still keep the skill of fishing from cut holes on ice-covered waters inherited from their ancestors. Daurs are also good at making carts with giant wheels, which are quite strong and handy, good for herdsmen who move from place to place.

The Daurs have their own spoken language but not a written one. In the Qing dynasty Daurs used the Manchu language. Now they read and write Chinese, and some also use the Mongolian, Uygur and Kazak languages.

In the past most Daurs believed in Shamanism and some in Lamaism, but now religious activities are rare. The Daurs respect the elderly; they are courteous, keen to help others, and warm to guests. The most important festival is the annual Anie, somewhat like the Spring Festival of the Han people. During holidays songs and dances are indispensable. In the long cold winter days, Daurs play a game similar to modern hockey.

Ewenki

The Ewenkis, population: 30,500 (2000 census). Most Ewenkis live in Inner Mongolia, and some in Heilongjiang and Xinjiang. Ewenki Autonomous Banner of Inner Mongolia Autonomous Region is the largest Ewenki community.

Ewenki, the name of their own, means "people living in forests in big mountains." Due to migration in history, Ewenkis lived in scattered communities in different stages of economic and social development. In the 1950s most Ewenkis engaged in animal husbandry and agriculture, and some lived on hunting. At that time they were still in the late stage of primitive society. In 1965 nomadic Ewenkis settled down in Aoluguya in Inner Mongolia, where an Ewenki township was established. Many people in the township still lived on hunting or raising reindeer, and they were known as "the last hunting tribe in China."

Ewenki children and a reindeer.

The Ewenkis have a spoken language but not a written one. Ewenkis in pastoral areas now use Mongolian and Chinese, and those in agricultural and mountain areas use Chinese. Ewenkis are good at making daily use articles out of birch bark, and they now make birch-bark craftworks.

Ewenkis believe in Shamanism, and Ewenki herdsmen also believe in Lamaism. They are good singers and dancers, and they have many festivals, such as the Spring Festival, the Aobao (heaps of stones used by the Mongolians and Tibetans as markings for roads or boundaries) gatherings for sacrifice, and the Mikuole festival celebrating harvests. Now Aobao gatherings have become recreational activities.

Oroqen

The Oroqens, population: 8,200 (2000 census). The Oroqens mainly live in Inner Mongolia and Heilongjiang, and Oroqen Autonomous Banner of Inner Mongolia is their major compact community.

Oroqen hunters.

For generations Oroqens lived in the forests of Greater and Lesser Hinggan Mountains, and made a living by collective hunting, and also collecting and fishing, with yields and catches equally shared. In the 1950s Oroqens began to shift to a settled life, engaging in farming and the forestry industry. In 1996 Oroqens imposed a ban on hunting, ending this centuries old way of life.

The Oroqens have their own spoken language, but not a written one. They usually use Chinese.

Oroqen craftsmanship is well known for making articles and even boats with birch-bark, and cutting beautiful designs on them. They are also good at processing hides. Their traditional garments are usually made of the skin of roe deer, which is warm and wearable. Their hats, made of a whole head skin of roe deer, serve as the best camouflage during hunting operations.

The Oroqens used to believe in Shamanism, and all gods of nature, including the god of mountain, god of sun, god of fire, and so on. They have an awe of the bear and tiger, and never call them by their names. They also practice ancestor worship. Oroqens respect the elderly and are warm to guests. They are also good at singing and dancing. The Oroqens celebrate the Spring Festival, Dragon Boat Festival, and the Mid-autumn Festival, due to the influence of the Han and other ethnic groups.

Hui

The Huis, population: 9,816,800 (2000 census), the third largest among the 55 minorities in China. Hui people can be found in most counties and cities in China. Ningxia Hui Autonomous Region is the largest Hui community in the country, and there are smaller communities of Hui people in various parts of China.

The earliest Hui people in China were the descendants of Arabs and Persians who came to China for trade in the seventh century. In the 13th century, a large number of Moslems moved to China from Central Asia and merged with the Han, Uygur, Mongolian and other ethnic groups, and finally the Hui ethnic group was formed. Traditionally Hui people were good traders. Those who live in agricultural and pastoral areas engage in agriculture and animal husbandry, and also take retailing and handicraft as sidelines. Urban residents of the Hui ethnic group usually engage in trade and catering, and those along the coast go in for offshore trade and fishery.

The Hui people use Chinese as their own language. As they live together with the Han and other ethnic groups, their garments are much the same as local people of other ethnic groups. Hui people pay special attention to cleanness of clothes and houses, and males usually wear white caps. The Huis believe in Islam, and their customs are influenced by the religion. They do not eat pork, and usually do not smoke or drink alcohol. Their major festivals include the Lesser Bairam and Qurban. The Lesser Bairam marks the end of Ramadan, a month-long fast held from sunrise to sunset. On the Qurban, Moslems go to mosques for collective prayers, and then they slaughter cattle and sheep to celebrate the festival.

Hui Moslems.

Uygur

The Uygurs, population: 8,399,400 (2000 census). The Uygurs reside mainly in Xinjiang Uygur Autonomous Region.

Uygur, the ethnic group's own name, means "unity" or "alliance" in the local language. Uygurs used to lead a nomadic life. After the mid-ninth century, they shifted to agriculture, mainly oasis farming and gardening, and also raising livestock. Uygurs have a superb craftsmanship and a tradition of trading. Their craftworks include carpets, tapestries, embroidery, embroidered caps, jade carvings, knives, and ethnic musical instruments.

The Uygurs have their own spoken and written language. They love literature and art, and have special art talents. They have many narrative poems, folklores and folk songs. Uygurs also have many musical instruments. Uygur men and women, old and young, are good at singing and dancing. Their dances feature movements of the neck and whirls. Their craftworks are also peculiar.

A Uygur woman.

Uygurs have flour as their staple food, and they also love beef and mutton. The typical Uygur garment for men is a long gown, and for women, a vest over a one-piece dress. All Uygurs, old and young, men and women, like to wear an embroidered cap. Uygurs are warm-hearted, and they pay special attention to courtesy in treating guests and visiting others.

The Uygurs are Islam believers. Their traditional festivals include the Lesser Bairam and Qurban. In holidays they not only sing and dance, but also hold various recreational activities, such as seizing sheep, wrestling, skating, and skiing.

Kazak

The Kazaks, population: 1,250,500 (2000 census). The Kazaks mainly live in Ili Kazak Autonomous Prefecture of Xinjiang. Most Kazaks engage in pasturing, and some in agriculture or both agriculture and animal husbandry. Kazak herdsmen used to move from place to place, living in movable yurts in spring, summer and autumn, and moving in earth or wood houses in winter. Now most Kazaks have settled down. Historically Kazaks believed it was immoral and infamous to trade. Now many people have given up this old concept.

Kazaks have their own spoken and written language – a writing system using Arabic letters. Still circulating are many ancient Kazak poems, folklores and proverbs. Kazaks are good singers and dancers, and at celebrations musical dialogue is a must. Excellent singers and superb craftsmen are widely respected. Kazaks are very hospitable. They pay special attention to birth and wedding celebrations. In daily life they drink wine made of horse milk and tea with milk.

Kazak people believe in Islam. Apart from the common festivals for Moslems, they also celebrate Noroz, which is similar to the Spring Festival of the Han people, bidding farewell to the past year and ushering in a new year. Traditional recreational activities include horse racing, "girl-chasing", seizing sheep, and singing while playing a musical instrument.

Kazaks – man and women.

Kirgiz

The Kirgizs, population: 160,800 (2000 census). The Kirgiz people in China reside mostly in Kizilsu Kirgiz Autonomous Prefecture of Xinjiang.

Kirgizs are mostly a pastoral people, with some engaging in agriculture full-time or part-time. Their lifestyle is somewhat nomadic.

Kirgizs are good at singing and dancing. In Kirgiz literature and art, the most salient are folk songs, poems and music. *Manas*, one of the three heroic epics of ethnic minorities in China, is an encyclopedia of the ethnic group, including its history, language, music, geography, religion and folkways. Among Kirgiz craftworks the most well known are embroidery and knit articles. The favorite color for Kirgiz people is red, and their garments and craftworks are all decorated in red.

Kirgiz women.

Kirgizs have their own spoken and written language, and in some areas they also use the Uygur and Kazak languages. Most Kirgizs believe in Islam, and some in Lamaism. As they live a nomadic life, there are not many mosques, and they do not observe the religious rituals as strictly as other people who live a settled life.

Kirgizs are very hospitable, and they treat all guests, familiar or not, warm-heartedly. Their major festivals include Norouz, Lesser Bairam, and Qurban. The Norouz is the celebration of the New Year, on which all Kirgiz households prepare feasts to treat each other. During the holiday, they will hold recreational activities such as singing and dancing, seizing sheep, horse racing, and wrestling.

Xibe

Xibe youths.

The Xibes, population: 188,800 (2000 census). The Xibe people dwell mainly in Xinjiang and the Northeast.

For generations Xibe people lived in the Northeast, later some of them migrated to Xinjiang. The Xibes used to live on hunting and fishing, and later shifted to agriculture. The Xibes in Xinjiang still keep their own spoken and written language, and they also use the Chinese, Uygur and Kazak languages. The Xibes in the Northeast have adopted the language, food and lifestyle of the local Han and Manchu people.

Xibes attach great importance to culture and education, and they have a talent for languages. Many Xibe people have a mastery of a number of languages, and they engage in translation, publishing and teaching. In Xibe literature, most are translated works.

Xibes used to despise commerce, but this mentality has now changed. Xibe people still value filial piety, respect for the elderly, and willing to help others. They are good at singing and dancing, love riding horses, archery, and wrestling. Quite a few Xibe archers have taken part in national and international sports games.

Xibe people used to be believers of Shamanism, and some also believe in Lamaism. They highly value ancestor worship. Xibe folk festivals are much the same as those of the Han people. Xibes in Xinjiang set the 18th day of the fourth month in the Chinese lunar calendar as the Westward Migration Day.

CHINA

Tajik

The Tajiks, population: 41,000 (2000 census). The Tajiks in China mainly reside in Taxkorgan Tajik Autonomous County of Xinjiang.

For generations Tajiks live in valleys at an altitude of about 3,000 m above sea level. They engage in pasturing plus farming, and live a semi-nomadic, semi-settled life.

Tajiks have their own spoken language but not a written one, and use the Uygur language instead. They worship the mountain eagle, and many of their dances mimic the movements of the eagle. Even their piccolo, which is used for accompaniment of dancing, is made of bones of the eagle.

Tajik youths playing the piccolo.

Tajik garments are relatively simple for men, and colorful for women. Tajik women like to wear red or colored one-piece dress with laces and a vest over it, and a round embroidered cap. They are good at knitting, sewing and embroidery.

Tajik people are honest and sincere, and warm-hearted. They give warm reception alike to visiting guests or strangers who ask for help. At dinner they would have the seats of honor reserved for the elderly and guests, and others would sit around.

The Tajiks believe in Islam, but they usually pray only on holidays. Apart from Moslem holidays, they also celebrate their Spring Festival in March. At the festival they would clean houses to welcome a new year and spread flour to pray for good harvests. During the holiday they would hold recreational activities, such as singing and dancing, seizing sheep, games on horseback, and other sports.

Uzbek

An Uzbek girl.

The Uzbeks, population: 12,400 (2000 census). The Uzbeks in China mainly reside in Xinjiang Uygur Autonomous Region.

Most Uzbeks live in cities and towns, engaging in commerce and the handicraft industry. Some go in for animal husbandry and agriculture. As they have long lived together with the Uygur people, they have taken up the lifestyle, folkways and religion of the Uygurs.

The Uzbeks have their own spoken and written language, and many people also know the Uygur or Kazak languages. They pay special attention to rearing children. When a baby is born, the family would hold a ceremony and give a feast to guests. Uzbek elderly people are widely respected.

Uzbek men and women wear traditional embroidered caps. Uzbek women are good at embroidery, and they like to embroider various patterns on garments and other daily use articles.

Uzbeks love singing and dancing, and they have rich folk music, including folksongs, ballads, and classical music. Their musical instruments are mainly plucking and percussion instruments.

Uzbek people believe in Islam, and their festivals are mostly religion-related. The most important ones are the Lesser Bairam and Qurban.

Russian

The Russians, population: 15,600 (2000 census). The Russians in China mostly live in Xinjiang, and the rest in Inner Mongolia, Heilongjiang and other places.

Russians moved from Russia to China in the late 18th century. Previously Russians in cities and towns engaged in repairing, transport and handicraft industries, and those in the countryside formed their own villages of several dozen households, engaging in farming, pasturing, or gardening.

The Russians in many ways keep their lifestyle from Russia, but the Han and other ethnic groups have also greatly influenced them. Their staple food is homemade bread and Russian dishes. Their garments are mostly modern.

A Russian girl.

The Russians pay high attention to education, and they have many intellectuals, engaging in culture, education, and technical professions. Russians have their own language. They use Russian at home or between kinsmen, but other commonly used languages in the localities when they deal with people of other ethnic groups.

Russians are highly courteous in receiving guests. Most Russians go to the Orthodox Church, and some are

Christian. The major festivals for Russians are Easter and Christmas, both related to religion.

Tatar

The Tatars, population: 4,900 (2000 census). The Tatars in China mainly live in cities and towns in Xinjiang.

Tatars in China originated from Europe, and they still keep some European way of life. They usually live in separate houses, with a firewall or fireplace inside. They use carpets and tapestries, and their furniture is usually European. Tatars often prepare European snacks for holidays or guests. At dinner they usually use spoons rather than chopsticks.

Tatar youths.

Tatars have a tradition in commerce. They have their own spoken and written language, and also use Uygur and Kazak. They pay high attention to education, and among them are many intellectuals.

Tatars are good singers and dancers. Some Tatar songs and dances have prevailed in Xinjiang, where nearly all celebrations including weddings, of any ethnic group, would have such songs and dances.

Tatars believe in Islam. They celebrate similar Islamic festivals as other local minorities do. Their peculiar festival is the Plowshare Festival, which usually falls in June. During the holiday, Tatars will wear ethnic costumes, sing and dance, and hold sports activities such as horse racing, tug-of-war, and wrestling.

Dongxiang

A Dongxiang girl.

The Dongxiangs, population: 513,800 (2000 census). The Dongxiangs mainly reside in Dongxiang Autonomous County of Linxia Hui Autonomous Prefecture in Gansu Province, and a small number of them live in Qinghai Province, Ningxia Hui Autonomous Region, and Xinjiang Uygur Autonomous Region.

Most Dongxiangs engage in agriculture, and some in animal husbandry, especially raising sheep. Now every year quite a few Dongxiang people go to other parts of the country to work in catering, transportation and other industries.

The folkways and religion of Dongxiang are similar to the Hui in northwest China. They still kept traditional garments in the early 20th century, but nowadays their garments are similar to those of the Han and Hui people in the locality, with some difference in their headwear. Dongxiang people treat guests warmly, and their traditional food for guests is chicken.

Dongxiangs speak their own language, but they have no written language. Most Dongxiang people also use Chinese. They love singing the "Huaer" folksongs, which are resounding and full of ardor, and an important way for youths to express their love. Prevailing among Dongxiang people are also a large number of narrative poems and folklores. During slack season in farming, people would hold recreational and sport activities.

Dongxiangs believe in Islam, and their festivals are mostly religion-related.

Tu

The Tus, population: 241,200 (2000 census). The Tus mainly reside in Qinghai Province.

The Tu people were pastoral in history. Later they shifted to agriculture, taking pasturing as a sideline. They are also good at gardening, wool weaving and embroidery.

In the past the Tu people had their own spoken language but not a written one, and for quite a long time they have been using Chinese and Tibetan. In 1979 a written Tu language system was worked out, which is now in trial use.

An embroidered high collar is mounted on Tu garments for both men and women, and colorful-sleeve blouses are typical for females. Their staple food includes Qingke barley, wheat and potato. They like tea with milk, large pieces of cooked meat, and parched flour with butter, the typical foods for herdsmen. Tu people are hospitable, and in receiving a guest or seeing the guest off they would present three cups of wine to the guest. They often sing songs when drinking wine.

A Tu woman.

Tu people like singing and dancing. Their folksongs are divided into indoor and outdoor ones. The indoor ones are sung at various ceremonies, and the outdoor ones are mostly love songs, known as "Huaer."

Tu people are believers of Tibetan Buddhism. They have many festivals. The Nadun festival celebrating good harvests are held in village communities in late summer, lasting for nearly two months. During the holiday, people have horse racing, wrestling, "Huaer" folksongs, and also trade fairs.

Salar

The Salars, population:104,500 (2000 census). The Salar people in China mainly reside in Xunhua Salar Autonomous County of Qinghai Province.

A scene from a Salar opera.

The traditional mode of production for the Salar people is agriculture, and they also engage in gardening, felling, and leather processing. Families of close kinship usually live in the same place. Their housing is of a Central Asian style.

Salar people believe in Islam, and their folkways are similar to those of the Hui people in the locality. Salar men wear a white or black round cap, and women, a headscarf, with its color varying for women of different age groups. Salars like tea with milk and wheat tea, and they have their special ways of preparing and serving tea. Their wedding ceremonies also have peculiar rituals.

Salars have their own spoken language but not a written one. They use Chinese instead. Quite a few of them also speak Chinese or Tibetan. There are many Salar folk stories. They like singing folksongs, especially lyrics. Their most peculiar musical instrument is Kouxi, a small copper or silver device that produces touching sounds. Salar women like this device very much. They are also good at embroidery and paper-cut.

Major Salar festivals include the Lesser Bairam and Qurban.

Bonan

The Bonans, population: 16,500 (2000 census). The Bonan people mainly live in Bonan-Dongxiang-Salar Autonomous County of Gansu Province.

Bonan people have agriculture as their traditional mode of production, and also have animal husbandry and handicraft as sidelines. They have a superb craftsmanship of making dagger knives, which are sharp and durable, with beautiful handles. In other countries such knives are known as Bonan knives.

A Bonan woman.

Bonans practice Islam, and their folkways are greatly influenced by the religion. Bonan men usually wear a white round cap, and women, a headscarf, with different colors for different age groups. Their staple food includes flour and rice, and they also eat beef and mutton and drink tea.

Bonans have their own spoken language but not a written one. Most Bonans also speak Chinese. Almost all Bonans sing "Huaer" folksongs, and they have special music for weddings, which are usually grand events. In traditional Bonan sports are some elements of Mongolian herdsmen, such as riding, shooting, and wrestling.

Of the Bonan festivals, most are related to Islam, such as the Lesser Bairam and Qurban. Not religion-related are the Spring Festival and a few others.

Yugur

The Yugurs, population: 13, 700 (2000 census). Most of the Yugurs live in Sunan Yugur Autonomous County of Gansu Province.

A Yugur girl.

Yugurs were traditionally pastoral, living in tents. Now most of the herdsmen have settled down, and some have shifted to agriculture or the tourism industry.

The Yugurs practice Lamaism, and their folkways are similar to those of the Tibetans. The Yugur staple food is butter, zanba or roasted qingke barley flour, and milk products in pastoral areas, and grain and vegetables in farming areas. Yugurs serve best food at festivals or to guests, with wine following tea. They usually treat guests with large slices of cooked mutton. Yugur women wear caps with colorful decorations, with different caps for married women and unmarried girls.

Yugurs speak their own language but use Chinese as their written language. Yugur people have rich folklore, and they also love to sing and dance. Every year they will hold a grand horseracing event.

Tibetan

The Tibetans, population: 5,146,000 (2000 census). The Tibetans mainly live in Tibet Autonomous Region, and in neighboring provinces of Qinghai, Gansu, Sichuan, and Yunnan.

Tibetan women with hand prayer wheels in their hands.

The Tibetans mostly reside on the Qinghai-Tibet Plateau, with an average altitude of over 4,000 m above sea level. Their traditional economic activities are animal husbandry and agriculture.

Tibetan folkways are quite remarkable, including their food, garments, housing, weddings, funerals, rituals, and festivals. Many of them are still kept intact. Their staple food is zanba or roasted qingke barley flour, beef, and mutton. They like buttered tea and qingke wine. Their traditional garments feature long sleeves, loose waist, and wide front. At ceremonies, Hada, a piece of silk, is often presented as a gift. Tibetans are good singers and dancers. Tibetan is the spoken and written language of Tibetans. The Tibetan people have also scored remarkable achievements in literature, opera, drama, painting, sculpture, architecture, and medicine, with peculiar Tibetan characteristics. The Tibetan epic King *Gesar* is one of the three major heroic epics of China's ethnic minorities, and the longest epic in the world. The Potala Palace and the Jokang Temple in Tibetan capital Lhasa are inscribed on the World Heritage List.

The Tibetans believe in Tibetan Buddhism, and there are Buddhist temples everywhere in Tibet. Many of the Tibetan festivals are related to religion.

Major traditional Tibetan festivals include the Tibetan New Year, Xodoin, and Ongkor. The New Year in the Tibetan calendar is the most important festival of the year. Xodoin means yoghurt banquet, and it has become an event of Tibetan drama performances. Ongkor, or the harvest festival, is celebrated in farming areas.

Monba

The Monbas, population: 8,900 (2000 census). The Monbas mainly reside in the southeast of Tibet Autonomous Region.

A Monba woman.

Monbas mainly engage in agriculture, taking animal husbandry and hunting as sidelines. They used many production tools made of wood till the 1950s. Monbas are good at making bamboo and rattan articles and wooden bowls, which are now sold as craftworks.

As they have long lived together with Tibetans, Monbas have many Tibetan influences in their folkways. In the past, rarely any visitor came to the Monba area due to obstruction of mountains, and the area was regarded as a mystery, with many religious legends about it. A Monba village usually has a dozen or several dozen households. In Monba families men and women are equal, and in some families women even hold the economic power.

Monbas have their own spoken but not written language, and most of them also use Tibetan. They have rich folklore, and are good singers and dancers. Their folksongs are mainly about love and wine.

Most Monbas believe in Tibetan Buddhism, and some practice a primitive religion. They use the Tibetan calendar, and celebrate the same festivals as Tibetans do. During the Tibetan New Year, the whole village will get together, singing, dancing, and performing Monba drama.

Lhoba

A Lhoba girl.

The Lhobas, population: 3,000 (2000 census). The Lhobas have the smallest population among China's ethnic minorities. They mainly live in the southeast of Tibet Autonomous Region.

Lhobas used to live in canyons of high mountains, where population is sparse and communication conditions are poor, and they have little exchange with other ethnic groups. By the mid-20th century, the Lhobas were still in the late stage of primitive society, practicing slash-and-burn farming, hunting, and collecting. Though their population was small, they belonged to different tribes.

Lhobas have their spoken but not written language, and a few of them use Tibetan. For quite a long time, they used a primitive way of cutting notches on wood and tying knots on ropes to record things.

The Lhoba area is no longer closed as the government has built roads and bridges for them. Also built for them are a school and a hospital. Lhobas have also learned many new production methods.

The Lhobas have rich folklore, including an epic about Lhoba history. They practice a primitive religion, worshiping gods of nature. A few Lhobas celebrate the Tibetan New Year as Tibetans do, but various tribes also have their own festivals and celebrate the New Year at different times, all after the busy farming season. Many tribes also keep their customs of tribe gathering, with families meeting for feasts and recreational activities. Some tribes have the habit of holding weddings during the New Year holidays.

Qiang

The Qiangs, population: 306,100 (2000 census). The Qiangs mainly live in compact communities in western Sichuan Province.

The Qiangs live on the eastern edge of the Qinghai-Tibet Plateau. Their major economic activity is agriculture, and their sidelines are animal husbandry and hunting.

Qiang people usually live together in Qiang villages. Their houses are usually three to four stories, built of earth and stone. The first or ground floor is used as cattle sheds, the second floor for people to live, and the upper floor, for storing grain. Qiang stonemasons are well known in nearby Tibetan and Han areas for their high skills. As the area is full of high peaks and gorges, cable bridges are built over rivers. In forests and on cliffs, plank roads are built.

Both Qiang men and women wear headbands. The typical garment for men is blue gown with a sheepskin vest over it. Women's garments are more colorful. Qiang women are good at cross-stitch work and embroidery. Their embroideries are colorful, with delicate patterns.

A Qiang girl.

Qiang people have their own spoken language but not a written one, and many also use Chinese. Qiangs are good singers and dancers. Their folk culture includes fairy tales, poems, music, and dances. Of their musical instruments, the Qiang flute is the most notable.

Qiangs practice a primitive religion, but some also believe in Tibetan Buddhism. They have their own calendar and festivals. Good wine is a must at Qiang feasts.

Yi

The Yis, population: 7,762,300 (2000 census). The Yi people live in the provinces of Yunnan, Sichuan and Guizhou, and Guangxi Zhuang Autonomous Region. Among them Yunnan has the largest Yi community.

The traditional economy of the Yi people is agriculture, and in some areas they also practice animal husbandry. The Yi ethnic group has many offshoots, with different ways of housing and different garments. Garments of Yi women keep many traditional features. Yi villages usually have 20 to 30 households each.

Yi people have their own spoken and written language. There are numerous Yi classics, involving philosophy, history, religion, and literature. The Yis are good singers and dancers. There are many Yi tunes, such as tunes for climbing mountains, welcoming guests, and marrying. Their dances are mostly collective ones, such as the Jumping under the Moon dance. Yi handicraft works include colored lacquer painting, embroidery, and silver decorations.

Yi girls.

Yi people practice nature worship and ancestor worship. In some areas of Yunnan and Guizhou, Yi people believe in Daoism and Buddhism. Traditional Yi festivals are many, and the grandest is the Torchlight Festival, which falls on the 24th day of the sixth month in the lunar calendar. During the festival, Yi people hold torches and set bonfires, singing, dancing, and hold other activities such as bullfighting, boating, and tug-of-war. Yi people like wine, and they usually treat guests with wine.

Bai

The Bais, population: 1,858,100 (2000 census). Most Bai people live in Dali Bai Autonomous Prefecture of Yunnan Province, and others reside in Sichuan, Guizhou, and Hunan.

The traditional economic activity of Bai people is agriculture, and in a few areas they also engage in animal husbandry and fisheries.

The Bais adore white color, and this is also reflected in their garments. Traditional Bai houses have many carvings on the gateway and paintings of landscape, flowers and birds on the walls.

Bai people have their own language, and most of them also use Chinese. Many Bai people are Buddhists. The city of Dali is praised as a city of literature due to its rich storage of works of literature, history, technology, and arts. There are also quite a number of historical relics and sites left over by ancient Bai people, such as the old town of Dali, and the thousand-year-old three pagodas of Chongsheng Temple. Most Bai people have a gift of singing and dancing, and many villages have their own stages. Bai people are quite hospitable. When a guest comes they would serve three rounds of tea: the first round tastes bitter, the second, sweet, and the third, lasting pleasant taste. The San Yue Jie (Third Month Fair) is the grandest of Bai festivals, held in the third month of lunar calendar each year. The fair is a great event for trade and entertainment, and also a good opportunity for young people to meet and date.

Bai women.

Hani

The Hanis, population: 1,439,700 (2000 census). The Hani people mainly live in the Ailao and Wuliang Mountains.

Hanis engage mainly in agriculture, and they are good at building terrace fields. Some terrace fields consist of several hundred terraces,

A Hani girl.

extending from the valley to the hilltops. Hanis are also skilled tea farmers. Their villages are mostly built at mid-hill, and their houses are made of earth walls, bamboo and wooden frames, and thatched roofs. The houses are of three stories: the first floor is used for keeping livestock, the second, for people to live and to store grain, and the third, as a storage.

Hanis have their own language. In 1957 a Hani writing system was created based on the Latin alphabet. Hani folk tales are numerous, some about the origins of all things, and some about the migration of Hani people. Hanis are good at singing and dancing, and most people carry musical instruments with them. They worship various gods and their ancestors, and value highly the births of babies and weddings of young people.

Traditional Hani calendar divides a year into three seasons: the cold season, warm season and rainy season. They celebrate two New Years a year, one in the tenth month, and the other in the sixth month. The tenth month New Year features a Street Feast, which is held in the main street and attended by the whole village.

Dai

The Dais, population: 1,159,000 (2000 census). The Dai people in China live mainly in Xishuangbanna Dai Autonomous Prefecture of Yunnan Province.

The traditional economic activity for the Dais is agriculture, especially growing rice.

Dai people live in two-story bamboo houses, a traditional Dai building. They live upstairs and keep livestock and store things downstairs. Dai garments are much the same for men in all areas, but somewhat different for women in various localities. What is common is that Dai women all wear their hair in a bundle, and that they wear pail-form skirt and short blouse. Different decorations usually signify different offshoots of the ethnic group.

The Dais have their own calendar and medicine. They like poems, especially narrative ones. Dai dances are numerous, and many mimic the movements of animals, such as the Peacock Dance.

Dai people practice Hinayana Buddhism. In history many monks were masters of Dai classics, including astronomy, calendar, and medicine. Locals believe these monks were the most learned. In Dai tradition, a period of religious life away from home is a must for young men to become civilized before they can marry.

A Dai girl.

The most important festival for the Dais is the Water-Splashing Festival, the New Year in the Dai calendar, which falls in mid-April. During the holiday they splash water on each other as a blessing, conduct dragon boat racing, sing and dance, and hold trade fairs.

Lisu

The Lisus, population: 634,900 (2000 census). The Lisus mainly live in Nujiang Lisu Autonomous Prefecture of Yunnan Province.

Lisus reside in an area in southwest China full of mountains and valleys, with poor communication conditions. Lisu villages are mostly situated halfway up mountain slopes, and few Lisu households live separately. By the 1950s, the Lisus still practiced slash-and-burn farming, supplemented by collecting and hunting. Now the local production, life and communication conditions have improved a great deal, but the Lisus still keep their ethnic characteristics.

The Lisus have their own language. They used to have a primitive writing system, and in 1957 a new written language was created adopting the Latin alphabet. Young and middle-aged Lisu people usually use Chinese. Their folk tales are numerous. There are about a dozen tunes in their folksongs, sung on different occasions, such as working in the fields, hunting, and building houses, with impromptus words. Their dances are mostly collective ones, stressing the movements of feet.

Lisu men.

In the past both Lisu men and women had the habit of chewing tobacco and drinking alcohol, but few women still keep this habit today. Lisus practice a primitive religion and nature worship. Some also believe in Catholicism or Christianity. Their traditional festivals include the New Year, Harvest Festival, Torchlight Festival, and the Climbing Knives Festival.

Va

The Vas, population: 396,600 (2000 census). The Va people mainly live in Ximeng Va Autonomous County and Cangyuan Va Autonomous County in southwestern Yunnan Province.

Va women.

Va people call themselves "Ah Vas", meaning "people who live in mountains." Traditionally Va people engaged in agriculture, plus hunting and collecting. In the 1950s they still practiced slash-and-burn farming. Their houses are usually two-story bamboo buildings, with simple furniture and a fire pit.

The Vas have their own language. Previously they had no writing system, and they recorded things by cutting notches on wood. In 1957 a written language based on the Latin alphabet was created. Va people are gifted singers and dancers, and they have rich folk tales. In the past they practiced a primitive religion, and paid homage to ghosts annually. The wood drum was a sacred utensil for such a ceremony. In the 1970s the drum was reformed to become a typical musical instrument of the Vas. In the meantime many activities of sacrifice have become entertainment activities.

Va people like alcohol, and they chew betel nuts. Alcohol is presented at festivals, weddings and funerals, and in receiving guests. Va people in some areas believe in Buddhism or Christianity.

Jingpo

The Jingpos, population: 132,100 (2000 census). The Jingpos mainly reside in Dehong Dai and Jingpo Autonomous Prefecture of

Yunnan.

A Jingpo girl.

Most of Jingpo people live in mountain areas. Their traditional mode of production is agriculture, and they also engage in animal husbandry, collecting and the handicraft industry.

The Jingpo ethnic group has many offshoots. A Jingpo village usually has several dozen households, and some larger ones have over one hundred families. Most of the villages are built amid trees and bamboos. Their residential buildings are mostly two-story bamboo and wood structure; the first floor keeps livestock, and the second floor, for people.

The Jingpos have their own language. In 1957 a written language based on the Latin alphabet was created. Jingpo folk tales and ballads are quite rich, including narrative poems, fairy tales, and stories about the origin of the ethnic group, and their history of migration. Jingpo people have a gift of singing and dancing, and they sing and dance to hail good harvests, usher in the New Year, welcome guests, and at weddings and funerals.

Jingpos used to be polytheistic. Now some people are Christians, and others are Buddhists. Jingpos in Dehong hold a massive traditional song and dance event on the 15th day of the first month of the lunar calendar, to express their good wishes and celebrate good harvests.

Naxi

The Naxis, population: 308,800 (census). The Naxis mainly reside in Lijiang Naxi Autonomous County of Yunnan, and some live in Sichuan Province.

The traditional economic activity of Naxi people is agriculture, but Naxis in some areas also practice animal husbandry. Various Naxi areas are in different stages of economic and social development. After the 1950s modern industry was introduced to some areas. Naxi families are now mainly based on monogamy, but remnants of the primitive maternal marriage system are still found in some places.

Naxi girls.

The Naxi people have rich cultural heritage, including the Dongba characters, known as "the only live pictographs in the world;" the Naxi ancient music, which was inherited from central China but has disappeared there; the native Dongba religion; and the Old Town of Lijiang, a site on the World Heritage List.

The Naxis have their own spoken and written language, but they commonly use Chinese as they have had close contacts with the Han people. The ancient Dongba characters are used mainly by Dongba priests writing scriptures. The Dongba scriptures are regarded as an encyclopedia of ancient Naxis. Naxi folk culture combines poems, music and dance.

Naxis practice the Dongba religion and Tibetan Buddhism. Apart from festivals of the Han people, Naxis also have a number of their own traditional festivals, such as tasting new harvests, paying homage to mountains, meeting in the third month, and the Torchlight Festival.

Lahu

The Lahus, population: 453,700 (2000 census). The Lahus mainly reside in Lancang Lahu Autonomous County of Yunnan Province.

The area inhabited by Lahus is mountainous, and their traditional economic activity is agriculture, plus seasonal hunting and collecting. Till the 1950s they still practiced slash-and-burn farming, and some even engaged in primitive collective farming, with all members sharing the harvests. Their handicraft industry produced ironware, textile fabrics and bamboo articles for their own use. Now things have changed greatly, but Lahu people still keep many of the traditional customs in their weddings, funerals, and festival activities.

The Lahus have their own language, but they also use Chinese and Dai, due to their long contacts with the Han and Dai ethnic groups. In 1957 a written Lahu language was created.

Lahus adore black, and they like black garments. They are good singers and dancers, and have many folk tales. Lahus take the gourd as their symbol, and the Lusheng, a wind instrument made of gourd, is typical of Lahu music. They also have the traditional Lusheng dance.

Lahu women.

Lahus used to be nature worshipers, but now among them are Buddhists, Christians, and Catholics. They like alcohol, and whenever they drink they would sing.

Their traditional festivals include the Spring Festival, Torchlight Festival, and the Festival for Tasting New Fruits.

Blang

The Blangs, population: 91,900 (2000 census). The Blangs mainly live in mountains in Menghai County of Xishuangbanna, Yunnan Province.

A Blang girl.

Blangs mainly engage in agriculture, planting cotton and tea. Menghai is one of the producing areas of Pu'er tea, one of the noted teas in China. Now tea is a major source of revenues for the Blang people. Blangs like chewing sour tea leaves, and Blang women are skilled tea producers. Blangs are good drinkers of alcohol, and they usually make the beverage at home.

Blangs live in their own villages. Their houses are mostly two-story piled buildings, with livestock kept downstairs. Their garments are mainly of blue and black. Blang men wear tattoos, and women, pail-form skirts, earrings, chokers, and bracelets.

Blangs have their own spoken language but not a written one. Some Blang people speak Dai, Va or Chinese, and use Chinese or Dai writing systems. Blang folk tales are many. Blang people like singing and dancing, and in holidays they would sing and dance to their hearts' content. Blang men love martial arts.

Most blangs believe in Hinayana Buddhism. The Hounan festival is a grand event for Blangs, held in the middle of the fourth month in the lunar calendar.

Achang

Achangs, population: 33,900 (2000 census). Achang people mainly live in Dehong Dai and Jingpo Autonomous Prefecture of Yunnan Province.

Achangs mainly engage in agriculture, especially rice farming. Achangs live in their own villages among local Tai, Han and other ethnic groups. Their houses are usually two-story brick or stone structure, with livestock kept downstairs.

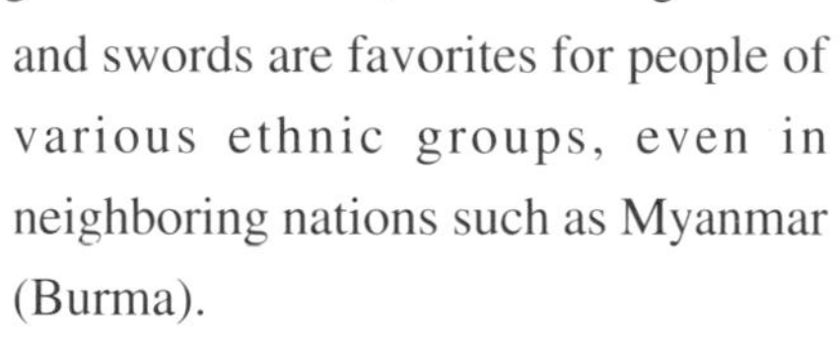

Achang garments are neat and simple. Men carry a bag and an Achang sword, and women have different garments before and after marriage. Achang people are good blacksmiths; their Achang knives and swords are favorites for people of various ethnic groups, even in neighboring nations such as Myanmar (Burma).

An Achang girl.

Achangs have their own spoken language but not writing system. As they live among Han and Dai people, most Achang men also speak Chinese and Dai, and some also speak Burmese and Jingpo. There are many Achang folk tales and songs. Young people often sing their love to their loved ones. Among Achang dances, the Elephant Leg dance and Monkey dance are most popular.

Achang people in some areas

practice a primitive religion, and those in other areas believe in Hinayana Buddhism. Their major festivals include the Torchlight Festival and the Woluo Festival. The Woluo, held on the fourth day of the first month in the lunar calendar, is in memory of the legendary first ancestor of Achang.

Primi

The Primis, population: 33,600 (2000 census). The Primis live mainly in mountain areas in northwestern Yunnan Province. Their traditional economic activity is agriculture, but they also engage in animal husbandry and the handicraft industry. They have a gift of making homemade cloth, bamboo woven articles, and lacquer bowls.

A Primi girl.

Primi villages are usually situated halfway up mountain slopes, with kinfolks living together in compounds. Their houses are mostly of wood structure, with people living upstairs. The family members often gather around the fire pit in the house. Primis adore white, and their garments are mostly in this color. They respect the elderly and love the young, and they are very hospitable. In history Primis despised traders, believing it was immoral to trade. But there are now quite a few Primis engaging in transport and retailing business.

Primis have their own language, but they usually use the Chinese writing system. They love songs and dances, and they hold dialogues in songs on major events including weddings and funerals.

Primis practice nature worship, and a few also believe in Lamaism and Daoism. The grandest festival is the Spring Festival, when they pay homage to ancestors, have a New Year feast, hold a ceremony for children who reach 13 for them to enter puberty, and conduct other recreational activities. Primis have a festival of climbing mountains, in which they camp on mountains around bonfires, singing and dancing.

Nu

The Nus, population: 28,800 (2000 census). The Nus mainly reside in Nujiang Lisu Autonomous Prefecture of Yunnan Province.

The Nu people live amid high mountains and valleys. The landscape and folkways are attractive to tourists, but the poor soil and communication conditions are not fit for people. Till the 1950s the Nus still practiced slash-and-burn farming, and kept records of things in primitive ways.

A Nu girl.

Nu villages are mostly halfway up the mountains, with kinfolks living together. Nu women's garments keep more traditional features than men's. Nu people used to slide along cables made of thin bamboo strips across valleys. Now modern bridges have been built, and the cables – now steel ones – are still there.

Nus have their own spoken language, but with highly different dialects. They have no written language, and use Chinese instead. Nu folk tales have many poems, mostly impromptus ones. Their dances are mostly imitations of animal movements and production activities. Nus love alcoholic beverage, and they are also good at making the beverage.

Nus used to practice a primitive religion. Those who live near Tibetans have taken up Tibetan Buddhism, and there are also some Catholics and Christians. Nu festivals include the New Year, Flower Festival, and festivals for paying homage to the God of Grain and to mountains and forests.

De'ang

The De'angs, population: 17,900 (2000 census). De'angs live in Yunnan Province.

De'angs engage in agriculture, especially growing tea. For generations De'angs have been known as excellent tea farmers. Tea is their major source of revenue. They love tea, and also use tea as a gift in receiving guests, in proposing a marriage or in settling disputes. They are also good at making bamboo and pottery articles.

A De'ang girl.

De'angs live sparsely, among Han, Dai, Jingpo and Va people. They are greatly influenced by the Dai, and their religion and folkways are much similar to those of the Dai. They live in piled buildings made of bamboo.

De'ang people have their own language, and some also use Dai, Chinese or Jingpo. They have rich folk tales and ballads. Their music is mainly percussion music, and their "water drum" is quite peculiar – the drum is made of ox hide and wood, and filled with some water when beating. De'angs dance at religious festivals. They have a brilliant history of architecture and sculpture, and ruins of ancient De'ang palaces and walls still exist in some places.

De'ang people practice Buddhism, and every village has a Buddhist temple. The grandest annual event is the Water-Splashing Festival, when people wash Buddhist statues and splash water at each other as New Year blessings.

Derung

The Derungs, population: 7,400 (2000 census). The Derungs mainly live in the Derung River valley in northwestern Yunnan Province.

Due to the high altitude, the mountains in the area inhabited by the Derungs are snow-clad half a year, and the place is hard to access. Therefore the Derung valley is also know as a "mysterious valley." Till the mid-20th century, the ethnic group was still in the process of dissolution of primitive society. People lived on planting crops, hunting and collecting. Women had tattoos on their faces.

Derungs built their villages on the mountain slopes along the river. They live in bamboo or wood structure houses, with at least two fire pits in the house. One fire pit is for a small family, for the children of a family will not leave the family after marriage. The Derung tapestry is a peculiar article for the Derungs. Made of cotton or ramie threads dyed in five colors, the tapestry is used as a mantle in the day and a quilt in the night. Now it is used as an artwork.

The Derungs are gifted singers and dancers. They have their own spoken language but not a written one. Some Derungs use Chinese. Derungs still keep their ancient honest folkway: they believe all things have their owners, and they will not pick up anything lost on the road.

A Derung girl.

The Derungs used to practice a primitive religion of nature worship. Their traditional annual festival falls on a day in the last month of the year, which is chosen by a village. During the festival, they have feasts, perform songs and dances, visit friends and relatives, and also have other ceremonial activities.

Jino

The Jinos, population: 20,900 (2000 census). The Jinos mainly live in Jino Township of Jinghong City in Xishangbanna Dai Autonomous Prefecture, Yunnan Province.

Jinos' traditional mode of production is agriculture. Till the early 1950s the Jinos were still in the process of dissolution of primitive society, and they practiced slash-and-burn farming. As for traditional handicraft, Jino women are good at spinning and weaving cloth, while Jino men make bamboo articles.

The Jino Mountain where people of the ethnic group reside is of a tropical climate, abounding with tea, bamboo and trees. The traditional Jino houses are piled buildings, with people living upstairs and their livestock kept downstairs. Jinos have a saying, "The Hans stir-fry, the Dais dip, and the Jinos pound their food." It means Han people like to stir-fry their dishes, Dai people like to dip their food in various sauces, while Jino people like to pound their food and dress it with sauces.

The Jinos have their own language but not a writing system. Their folk culture includes epics, tales and ballads. They love songs and dances, and they learn tunes in their childhood. Most Jinos can compose words impromptus, and engage in musical dialogue. The Jino people worship the sun, and the sun drum is their traditional utensil of sacrifice and also a musical instrument. The Sun Drum Dance is their typical dance.

Jino women.

Jinos celebrate their New Year holidays in the 12th month of lunar calendar, with the date decided by each village. They also have a grand festival for new harvest of rice.

Miao

The Miaos, population:8,940,100 (2000 census). Compact communities of Miao people are found in Guizhou, Yunnan and the western part of Hunan, as well as in Guangxi, Sichuan, Hainan and Hubei. Qiandongnan Miao and Dong Autonomous Prefecture of Guizhou Province is the largest Miao community in China.

Traditionally the Miaos have been an agricultural people. They usually live in villages of the same clan names; a small village may have 20 to 30 households, and a large one, up to a thousand households.

There are over 130 designs of Miao garments accompanied by different silver decorations – other ethnic groups in China rarely have so many varied clothing styles. The most noted among traditional Miao craftworks include cross-stitch works, embroidery, brocade, wax printing, and silverware. Many of them have become commodities on both home and overseas markets.

A Miao girl.

The Miaos have their own language, but communication among different Miao dialects is often difficult if not impossible. Quite a large part of Miao people also use Chinese. In 1956 a Miao writing system was created. Miaos have rich folklore, especially poems. They are gifted singers and dancers, and their typical musical instrument is Lusheng, a wind instrument. The Lusheng Dance is the most popular, which stresses the movements of legs and feet.

The Miaos used to worship nature and ancestors. Among them are a small number of Catholics and Christians. They treat guests with wine. The grandest Miao festival is Miao New Year, usually after autumn. On some festivals bull fighting (a bull fighting a bull) is performed.

Bouyei

The Bouyeis, population: 2,971,500 (2000 census). Compact

communities of the Bouyeis include Qiannan Bouyei and Miao Autonomous Prefecture and Qianxinan Bouyei and Miao Autonomous Prefecture in Guizhou Province, and they are also distributed in other areas of Guizhou and parts of Yunnan and Sichuan provinces.

Bouyei people usually live in villages of the same clan names by mountainsides and along rivers. A village may have a dozen or several dozen households, or even several hundred households. Their houses include piled buildings, ordinary brick houses, and stone slab houses.

Bouyeis engage in agriculture, especially rice farming. As a tradition, Bouyei men work in the fields while women work at looms. Their wax printing technique has a long history, and the patterns are uniquely their own. Their garments are mainly in blue and white.

Bouyei girls.

Bouyeis have their own language and use Chinese characters. In 1956 a Bouyei writing system was created based on the Latin alphabet. They have rich folklore, and the Bouyei drama is quite popular.

Bouyeis worship nature and their ancestors, and some are Catholics or Christians. Apart from the Spring Festival, Dragon Boat Festival and Mid-Autumn Festival, they have their own festivals in different areas. For instance, in Chabai of Xingyi County in Guizhou, there is a Chabai Folksongs Festival, which falls on the 21st day of the sixth month in the lunar calendar.

Dong

Dong girls.

The Dongs, population: 2,960,300 (2000 census). The Dong people are mainly distributed in various parts of Guizhou, Hunan, and Guangxi.

Dong people are traditional farmers, especially rice farming. A few of them work in the forestry industry.

Dong people built their villages by hillsides and rivers. Their houses are usually two- or three-story piled buildings. In the middle of the villages there are high drum towers, usually one for people of the same family name. A large village may have three or four such towers, which serve as centers for public activities. They are also landmarks of Dong villages.

Dong culture is marked by its architecture, music and poems. Their embroidery, fabrics, painting, sculptures and silverware are also quite remarkable. The Dongs have their own spoken language, and a writing system was created in the 1950s. Present-day Dong people usually use Chinese.

The Dongs have a saying, "Food nourishes the body, and songs nourish the mind." The Dong Great Song is a chorus with multiple voice parts and without conductor or accompaniment. The chorus takes at least three singers, who are strictly selected and have been trained since childhood. They also have the Dong drama, developed based on ballads.

Dong people have many traditional festivals and collective entertainment activities. The most important of Dong festivals is the Spring Festival, and others include the Dong New Year, the festivals of tasting new crops and paying homage to the God of Cattle.

Sui

The Suis, population: 406,900 (2000 census). The Suis mainly reside in Sandu Sui Autonomous County of Guizhou Province, and a small number of them live in Guangxi.

The Suis are an agricultural people, especially rice farming. Sui villages are mostly by hillsides and rivers, and they live in piled buildings. By the 1940s Sui men had taken the garments of the Han people, but Sui women garments still retain much of their own features. Sui women have a gift of weaving, embroidery and wax printing. Their Sui cloth had become famous a century ago.

Sui women.

The Suis have their own language, but the Sui writing system is mainly used in religious activities. Sui people now use Chinese characters. Their folklore is quite rich, especially poems. Sui people use poems and songs in dating, marriage, birthdays, reception of guests, and settlement of disputes. The best-known Sui dance is the Bronze Drum Dance. They have a 700-year-old unique technology of soybean milk printing in making Sui cloth.

Sui people are polytheistic, practicing nature worship. Of all Sui festivals, the Duan is the most important. During the festival, Sui people pay homage to their ancestors, visit friends and relatives, and sing and dance.

Gelao

A Gelao girl.

The Gelaos, population: 579,400 (2000 census). Most Gelaos live in western Guizhou Province, and some reside in Guangxi and Yunnan.

Gelaos are traditionally an agricultural people – they grow rice in plains and other dry crops in mountains.

In ancient times the Gelaos were a major ethnic group in southwest China, but they had to retreat to mountain areas after being defeated by other ethnic groups. Gelao communities are mixed with those of other minorities, and their garments and folkways are similar to local people. In history Gelao bronze wares were quite well known, but their bronze-processing technique has been lost.

Gelaos have their own spoken language but not a written one. Contemporary Gelaos use Chinese, and only a small number can speak their own language. Gelao folklore is quite rich, and their ballads are mostly sung in Chinese. Their folk drama uses wooden masks.

Gelaos practice a primitive religion, worshiping their ancestors and various things. Their festivals are much the same as those of the Han people, but apart from the Spring Festival they also celebrate the Gelao New Year, which falls on the third day of the third month in the lunar calendar. Gelaos respect the elderly and are hospitable. They make good wine, and treat guests with wine.

Zhuang

The Zhuangs, population: 16,178,800 (2000 census), the largest among minority populations in China. The Zhuangs reside mainly in Guangxi Zhuang Autonomous Region, and some live in Yunnan, Guangdong, Guizhou and Hunan.

The Zhuangs were traditionally an agricultural people, roughly at the same level of development of local Han people. Ancient Zhuang people mastered the technique of making bronze drums over 2,000 years ago, and over 500 such drums have been found. The drums are a treasure of ancient Zhuang culture. Also quite well known is Zhuang brocade, which was listed as a tribute to the emperor during the Ming dynasty (1368-1644). Learning to make brocade used to be a must for Zhuang women.

The Zhuangs have their own language, but they also use Chinese characters. Zhuang people are gifted singers, and they have Folksong Fairs during slack season in farming, on holidays, or major events such as weddings and funerals. The fair on the third day of the third month in the lunar calendar is the grandest, attracting thousands of people. Such a fair is also a venue for young people to meet and date, and also for trading in commodities. Zhuang folklore is quite rich, and the Zhuang drama is

Zhuang girls.

popular among local people.

Zhuangs share many festivals with the Han people, and the most important is the Spring Festival.

Yao

The Yaos, population: 2,637,400 (2000 census). The Yaos are mainly distributed in the mountain areas of Guangxi, Hunan, Yunnan, Guangdong, Guizhou and Jiangxi.

A Yao girl.

Yao people mainly engage in agriculture, taking forestry and hunting as sidelines. As Yao communities are widely distributed, they are in different stages of development. In the 1950s some Yao areas still practiced slash-and-burn farming, and primitive collective hunting. Yao people mostly live in their own villages, located on mountains. A Yao village may have several dozen households.

Yao women are skilled in weaving, dyeing and embroidery, and make fine brocade and garments. Yao garments are decorated with embroideries in five-color threads and various patterns. It is recorded in Chinese classics that "Yaos wear colorful garments." Various offshoots of Yao are identified by their garments, such as the White-Pant Yao, and the Indigo Blue Yao.

Yao people have their own language with many dialects. In some areas Yaos also use Chinese or Zhuang. They have no writing system, and use Chinese characters instead. Yaos are gifted singers and dancers, and have rich folklore.

Yao people worship nature and their ancestors. And in some areas people also practice witchery or Daoism. Apart from celebrating festivals of the Han people, Yaos also have their own holidays, such as the King Panhu Festival in memory of their first ancestor Panhu. The festival falls on the 16th day of the tenth month in the lunar calendar. Apart from paying homage to King Panhu, youngsters also meet and sing.

Mulam

The Mulams, population: 207,400 (2000 census). The Mulams mainly live in mountain areas in northern Guangxi Zhuang Autonomous Region, with 90% of them in Luocheng Mulam Autonomous County.

Mulams mainly engage in agriculture, growing rice and cotton. Their production techniques and tools are roughly the same as those of neighboring Han and Zhuang ethnic groups. Their other production activities include coal mining, iron making, and pottery.

A Mulam girl.

The area inhabited by the Mulams has a landscape similar to that of Guilin, the most scenic tourist attraction in southern China. Mulam people of the same kinship usually live in the same village. As the place abounds with blind coal, Mulam households burn the coal in brick-lined pits inside their houses for cooking and heating. Mulams adore blue, and their garments are usually this color, with small embroideries on the sleeves and trouser legs.

Mulams have their own spoken language, but most people also speak Chinese and Zhuang. They write in Chinese characters. They love folksongs, with folksong books in nearly every household and good singers in every village.

Mulam festivals are much the same as those of the local Han and Zhuang people. Walking on Slopes is a favorite activity for Mulams, when young people meet, sing and date.

Maonan

The Maonans, population: 107,200 (2000 census). The Maonans mainly live in Huanjiang County in northern Guangxi Zhuang Autonomous Region.

The area inhabited by Maonans is on the eastern slope of the Yunnan-Guizhou Plateau, where there are many dissolved caverns. As soil is limited, local people developed intensive farming, opening small plots of land on the mountains, which are just like delicate artworks. Maonans are an agricultural people, and their beef cattle sell well at home and abroad.

A Maonan girl.

Among Maonan craftworks are bamboo articles, stone carvings, and silver ware. The most noted is the colored bamboo hat, which is delicately woven and quite useful. Maonan stone carvings and woodcarvings are also remarkable. Stone materials are widely used in their houses and daily life. The carvings on tombstones are really artistic.

Maonans have their own spoken language but without a writing system. Most Maonan people also speak Zhuang and Chinese, and use Chinese characters. Their folklore is quite rich, with peculiar epics and folksongs. Their folksongs are often impromptus. Besides, they also have a Maonan drama.

Maonans are polytheistic, and influenced somewhat by Daoism and witchery. Their traditional festival activities include paying homage to gods and ancestors, and singing musical dialogue.

Gin

The Gins, population: 22,500 (2000 census). Gin people in China mainly live on three islets in the Beibu Gulf in Guangxi.

The area inhabited by the Gins neighbors Vietnam, from which ancestors of Gins immigrated to China in around the 16th century. The Gins are the only one among China's ethnic minorities that lives by the sea. Their traditional economic activity is seasonal fishing, supplemented by salt making and farming. Contemporary Gins engage in border trade, aquatic farming, tourism, and oceanic products processing.

A Gin girl.

The Gin people have their own language but not a writing system, and most Gins speak the Canton (Guangzhou) dialect of Chinese and use Chinese characters. Gin people love songs, including folksongs, love songs, marriage songs, fishing songs, and narrative songs. They have a peculiar musical instrument – the single-stringed Qin. Ha (meaning songs) singing, bamboo rod dancing, and the single-stringed Qin are regarded as the three pearls of Gin culture. The Gins sing at Ha pavilions, a unique building for Gins.

Most Gin people practice Daoism, and a small number are Catholics. Their traditional festivals are mostly the same as those of the Han people. The grandest of them is the Ha (Songs) Festival, at which Gins used to welcome gods and pay homage to their ancestors. Now the festival is mainly a recreational activity.

Tujia

The Tujias, population: 8,028,100 (2000 census). Compact communities of Tujias are found in Xiangxi Tujia and Miao Autonomous Prefecture of Hunan Province, and Enshi Tujia and Miao Autonomous Prefecture of Hubei Province. Some Tujias live in Sichuan Province.

A Tujia girl.

The areas inhabited by Tujias have beautiful scenery, and people there are traditionally agricultural. Tujias have their own spoken language, but most of them use Chinese. Tujia is only spoken in a few places in Xiangxi. As they have no writing system of their own, they use Chinese characters.

Most Tujias live in wood-structure houses, especially piled buildings. Tujia garments are mainly in red and blue, with colorful embroideries on the edges. Tujia brocade is one of the best in China; it is not only used by Tujias themselves, but also sold to people of other ethnic groups. Among Tujia craftworks, carvings, paintings, paper-cuts and wax printing goods are remarkable.

Tujias love songs. Their most popular dance is the Hand Waving Dance, and their dramas include the Maogusi and Nuo drama. Maogusi, meaning hairy ancient humans in Tujia, is a primitive drama for sacrifice, combining songs, dances, and drama. It takes 15 to 16 people to act, and the actors, their bodies covered with straw and leaves, imitate the movements of ancient people.

Tujias are polytheistic, and they worship their ancestors. The most important festival is the Tujia New Year, which is one day earlier than the Spring Festival of the Han people.

Li

The Lis, population: 1,247,800 (2000 census). The Lis mainly live in the central-south part of Hainan Island.

The Li people reside in the basins among mountains on the tropical island. Their traditional economic activity is agriculture, supplemented by hunting, fishing and collecting. In the 1950s most of the areas inhabited by Li people were roughly in the same stage of development as the Han people, but in high mountains there were some Li people who still lived a primitive life of collective farming.

Li people of the same kinship live together in boat-shape houses built with bamboo and wood. Unmarried young people would live in separate houses, some attached to the family house, and some in other places. But nowadays such a living habit is found only in some remote villages.

Li people are known for their spinning and weaving techniques. In the 15th century, Huang Daopo, a woman of the Han ethnic group,

Li girls.

came from the mainland to learn the techniques and passed them to people in eastern China's Jiangsu and Zhejiang provinces. Lis have their own language, but many also speak Chinese. A Li writing system was created in 1957, but people still use Chinese characters. Li folklore is quite rich, and Li people are gifted singers and dancers. The Bamboo Rod Dance is quite popular.

Li people share many festivals with the Han people. Among Li festivals, the grandest is the San Yue San (the third day of the third month in the lunar calendar). During the festival, young people sing and dance, and meet and date, and revel around bonfires the whole night.

She

The Shes, population: 709,600 (2000 census). The She people are distributed in the provinces of Fujian, Zhejiang, Jiangxi, Guangdong and Anhui.

The Shes, traditionally an agricultural people, live in hilly country in the southeastern part of China. Repeated migration in history resulted in sparse distribution of the She people. Usually there are a few to several dozen households in a She village among villages of Han people, and in other villages She and Han people live in a mixed pattern.

Nowadays the garments of She men are the same as those of Han people, but garments of She women in eastern Fujian and southern Zhejiang still keep to the traditional She style. The most salient is colored embroideries on their clothes and aprons, which symbolize the phoenix. She legends believe the ancestral home of Shes is at the Phoenix Mountain in Chaozhou, Guangdong Province.

The She people are good at weaving and embroidery. They have many daily use articles made of bamboo strips, and these articles are sold as artworks on home and overseas markets. The bamboo hat for She women is a typical one of them.

She women.

The Shes have their own spoken language but not a written one, and they use Chinese characters instead. They have rich folklore, especially folksongs. She people practice martial arts, including She boxing and stick acrobatic play. They also like to climb mountains in holidays in spring and autumn.

Gaoshan

The Gaoshans, with a population of over 300,000, live mainly in the mountain areas in the central part of Taiwan, the Zonggu Plain in the eastern part of the island, and Lanyu islet. In addition, about 4,500 Ganshan people reside in various parts of the mainland of China.

Before large-scale immigration of Han people in the 17th century, Gaoshans in Taiwan were still in primitive society. Gaoshans in mountain areas lived on hunting, and those in plains made a living by farming. Now they have a modern life.

The Gaoshan ethnic group has many offshoots or tribes. Previously the tribes formed their own communities, with a council of elders presiding over a community. In 1952 the Taiwan authorities enforced regional autonomy in the mountain areas, and divided the areas inhabited by Gaoshans into 30 townships, which have their own administrative organs. Gaoshan families, which used to have 50 to 60 people, have now become much smaller.

Gaoshan athletes at the national games of ethnic minorities.

Gaoshans speak their own tongue, but have no written language. They have rich folk tales. The Gaoshans are gifted singers and dancers. The most popular dances are the Pestling Dance and Long Hair Dance. The Pestling Dance originated from the work of pestling rice. At the peak of the Long Hair Dance, the dancers bow their bodies and their hair touches the ground. Gaoshan handicraft includes spinning, weaving, carving and pottery.

Traditional Gaoshan festivals are usually activities of sacrifice. There used to be over 70 sacrifice items for various tribes. Now they have been combined, and the most important ones include praying for sowing seeds, for security, for good harvest, and for bamboo rods.

Han

The Hans are the principal ethnic group in China. The Han

population totaled 1,159.4 million (those in Hong Kong, Macao and Taiwan not included), or 91.59% of the national total in the fifth national census in 2000. Han people live in all parts of the country as the most widely distributed ethnic group.

The Han people have scored great achievements in politics, economy, culture, arts, science and technology. Traditionally the Hans were an agricultural people, with men tending the fields and women working at looms. Their farming and handicraft techniques are highly developed. Among their noted achievements are irrigation, intensive farming, silk, and porcelain. They contributed the four inventions of paper, printing, the compass, and gunpowder to the world. Traditional Chinese medicine, wushu (martial arts), Peking opera, Chinese paintings, and Chinese calligraphy are known as quintessence of Chinese culture. Chinese classics are numerous, and Chinese folk arts are colorful, with various local characteristics. Traditional Chinese architecture, including residential buildings, gardens and imperial palaces, occupies a unique position in world architecture.

Han culture is the mainstream of traditional Chinese culture. Confucianism founded by Confucius became the dominant ideology as advocated by feudal rulers of various dynasties. And an education and examination system was founded based on Confucian classics. Confucian culture, with its moral values and doctrines of decorum, has had a great impact on the Chinese nation.

Chinese characters are among the most ancient writing systems in the world. Chinese has many regional variants or dialects, and the common speech is *Putonghua*, which is based on the northern dialects, with the Beijing dialect as the standard pronunciation.

The Han people pay special attention to food and cooking. Different regions have different cuisines, and the most well known are those of Sichuan, Guangdong, Shandong, and the lower reaches of the Yangtze and Huai rivers. Chinese tea and liquor have also a splendid history.

A Han mother and her child.

Han people have a strong sense of family values. They respect the elderly and love the young, and stress harmonious family life. The Hans used to believe the more children the happier the family, but this concept has changed.

Han people in different areas have different habits and customs in food, clothing, housing, weddings, funerals, and festival activities. A Chinese saying goes, "People ten *li* (half a kilometer) away have different habits, and 100 *li* away have different folkways." Now the habits and customs are mainly found in some rural areas.

Traditional Han festivals include the Spring Festival, Lantern Festival, Qingming, Dragon Boat Festival, Mid-Autumn Festival, and Double Ninth Festival (the ninth day of the ninth lunar month). The Spring Festival is the grandest, when people pray for good harvest and good luck in the coming year, and keeping away from evils. Major activities during the festival include sacrifice to ancestors, visiting friends and relatives, and various entertainments, such as dragon dance, lion dance, and *Yangge* (a folk dance). On the Lantern Festival, people eat dumplings made of glutinous rice served in soup, and guess riddles written on lanterns. The Qingming festival, a day in early April, is the time for people to worship at ancestral graves or "sweeping" the graves and go outing. For the Dragon Boat festival, people run boat racing and eat dumplings made of glutinous rice wrapped in bamboo or reed leaves. Mid-Autumn Festival is the time people enjoy the full moon and eat moon cakes, looking forward to family reunion. During the Double Ninth Festival, people climb mountains and view chrysanthemums, and many areas hold activities to pay respects to the elderly.

In Han folkways, red is the color for celebrations, such as birthday anniversaries, weddings, festivals, and opening ceremonies. Red lanterns and couplets written on red paper are for major festivals.

Only a small number of Han people believe in religion, but the Hans have an open attitude towards various faiths. Major faiths for Han people include Buddhism, Daoism, Catholicism, and Christianity.